MW00441357

Praise for *Meeting at C-Level*

"Having been in the live events business for more than 30 years I have seen my share of books on the topic of audience engagement and alignment. However, nothing I have read has been as successful as this one at succinctly describing the step by step process used to realize the maximum potential and ROI from a meeting. Everyone's greatest memories are from a live experience and a meeting is no different. Cheers to Eric Rozenberg for his crafty authorship on this topic. I view this publication as essential reading for not only the C-level executive but also anyone in the live events industry!"

Ken Sanders
President, Freeman

"Eric tells us how to make Meetings & Events a critical component of a strategy and not solely a gathering of individuals. A must read for Commercial and Communication leaders to know how to make Meetings & Events an investment instead of a cost."

Fabrice Chouraqui
President, Novartis Pharmaceuticals US

"Thank you for writing this book! Wish we'd had it years ago. It's just what this industry needed—and what should be required reading in all MBA and leadership programs. This book actually speaks to C-level executives, helping them understand why, when, and how to apply the strategic tool of face-to-face meetings, or perhaps more aptly, "impactful visceral brand experiences." It fills a long-standing void and connects the dots between meetings and events, and marketing and corporate brand transformation.

This book is not only timely but totally on point. The well-told stories of real-world, in-the-trenches experiences make this book not only a fascinating read but help any reader relate to the author's insights and be able to transform them into immediately actionable strategies and tactics.

I couldn't put it down—the stories and insights are that good."

Alexandra L. Wagner, CMM
Former Director of Meetings and Events; Chief
Purpose Ambassador; Marketing, SunTrust Bank

"Like a good wine... getting better with time, and leaving its owner with the challenge of betting on when to open the bottle... or of waiting some more time. With his extensive career in events, and whilst he is still so young at heart, Eric has taken the bet to 'open his bottle' now, and to offer us a gift with his book. One should not only expect to learn a number of useful tips with this pleasant reading, but also to... want to go and organize one's next event rapidly... with professional help obviously ;-).

Some of my favorites 'sips' of this gift:

- To a senior execs team: "take a piece of paper and write your objectives ... you're not aligned and you hope to align 10,000 people?": simplicity .... Efficiency and .... Courage!

- To a pharma CEO: "Set up an advisory board with people who ...... don't know about your business!!"! Bold and so useful!"

Philippe Mauchard
Partner McKinsey&Company, Co-Founder McKinsey Solutions and leader Scale Up Services Europe/Israel

"Having worked with clients for more than 25 years, I've seen time and again the key issue that Eric has identified in this book. Many executives want jump straight to the conclusion without considering the path of how to get there and why they are even on the road in the first place. Through insightful real world examples, based on his own vast experience, Eric thoughtfully and repeatedly illustrates the value of not just how, but why to hold a meeting. His book reminds us that aligning vision and purpose with a focus on the details can be the difference between a costly but meaningless event, and something that truly moves the needle and creates lasting value for your organization."

Aaron Lee
Founder & CEO, Illuminati Studios, President of
Entrepreneurs' Organization (EO) South Florida

"A cleverly written piece that uses a common sense approach to solving important, complex business issues. Eric draws from his past experience and shows how simple techniques can make a world of difference in your results. Planners can elevate their value by using the tips in the book to help their sponsors design meetings based on business objectives. Happy reading."

Cindy D'Aoust
President and CEO,
Cruise Lines International Association

"Leading organizations have demonstrated how face-to-face meetings and live customer events can be leveraged to increase revenues, improve productivity, and deliver positive bottom-line results. However, before investing in an event, corporate executives need to be thoughtful about the strategic purpose and desired outcomes of the meeting in order to maximize the ROI.

In his book, Eric Rozenberg, a seasoned strategic event-planning professional, provides an insightful and practical methodology for leveraging the value of meetings, brought to life through real-world case studies from his own vast experiences."

Paul Van Deventer
President and CEO, MPI
Meeting Professionals International

"Eric Rozenberg's ability to tie basic principles with storytelling is unique and extremely effective. While Eric and I have been long-time colleagues and collaborators, his influence spans the globe and he has been widely recognized throughout the meetings and events industry for his professionalism and strategic approach. I urge you to invest your time in reading this new book."

Deborah Sexton
President & CEO, PCMA
Professional Convention Management Association

"Eric Rozenberg brings a new approach to aligning your meetings with your organization's objectives. I have witnessed first hand how he applies it to Advisory Boards and the stories he shares in 'Meeting at C-Level' are great examples you can apply immediately in your role as a senior executive."

Don Welsh
President and CEO, DMAI
Destination Marketing Association International

"It continues to be my pleasure to be a great friend and professional colleague of Eric Rozenberg. Conferences, exhibitions, and events significantly support the growth of global economies, professional development, and societal enhancements. This book is a 'must-read" for all executives leading colleagues who plan and/or attend face-to-face engagements."

David Dubois, CMP, CAE, CTA, FASAE
President and CEO, IAEE
International Association of Exhibitions and Events

"If ...

If you don't need to understand how to save time or money, if you don't need to understand the critical steps to developing a gathering of clients, peers, or association members, or if you don't comprehend the value of face-to-face interaction, close this book, set it down, and walk away.

If you're still reading and if you've worked in any industry long enough that the prospect of an upcoming work-related meeting, celebration, or training conference creates audibly collective sighs or the tumbling of eyeballs rolling back among your teams that feign appreciation, but really ... really ... really they wonder if there isn't a better use of their time—do not worry. There is hope.

If you've longed to understand the methodology of meetings and events, and you've longed to grasp how their outcomes can yield comprehensive and lasting results that change culture, communication, and currency, but you cannot resign yourself to tactical discussions on what's on the menu—there is hope.

In short order, the following pages will offer you simple steps to guide your whole thought-process and are shared through real-life experiences from across the globe. Eric's explanation of the dynamics of how to prepare and execute meetings and events will become required reading for C-level executives, directors, seasoned event professionals, and those choosing to pursue experiential marketing and event careers.

If you're looking for a way to plan the success of your company, your career, and dramatically transform your current face-to-face interactions, then start reading ... AND remember ... keep it uniquely different!"

Kevin G. Kirby
2014–2015 Chairman of International Board of Directors of MPI, Former Head of Marketing and Sales at Hard Rock International

"Choose Chicago had the distinct pleasure of working with Eric in 2016 as the facilitator of our first client advisory board in 10 years. Eric's depth of industry knowledge, intellect, organization, and ideas led to an overwhelmingly successful board meeting. He was able to shape a board meeting that furthered Choose Chicago's strategic goals while ensuring the goals of our client advisory board members were also met. Eric received outstanding reviews from everyone on the board and from everyone with Choose Chicago."

Marc Anderson
Interim CEO, Chief Sales Officer and SVP,
Choose Chicago

"Eric has made a complex topic simple with this book. He lays out a set of simple steps that enable senior executives to grasp the key issues in event design. The book does a great job of making the 'business case' for designing intelligent, impactful meetings and events. I hope it becomes required reading in boardrooms globally."

Carl Winston
Director of L. Robert Payne School of Hospitality and Tourism Management, San Diego State University

"It becomes quickly clear when an event is being thoughtfully planned, based on vision, relevant matrix and organizational objectives rather than only feelings and tradition. The preparation, proceedings and the results improve dramatically.

Based on the title *Meeting at C-Level* had the potential to be important and is, in fact, excellent."

Brian Palmer, CMM
President, National Speakers Bureau

"Eric's question to the reader, 'Why are you holding this meeting?' hit home with me in a very big way. From a hotel's perspective, we can only meet the customer's expectations if we truly understand the goals. Creating a unique experience for the attendee must be the outcome. Face-to-face meetings are weaved through every bit of culture at Hyatt Hotels.

A great read with an extremely important message."

Gus Vonderheide
VP Global Sales, Hyatt Hotels

"Eric Rozenberg is truly a legend in the meetings and events industry. His book is a rare opportunity for the reader to benefit from his many years of experience and insights normally reserved for his valued clientele. As an executive trying to harness the power of face-to-face meetings, Eric's book is a must-read."

Vincent J. LaRuffa
Vice President, Resort Marketing and Sales,
Universal Orlando Resort

"Meeting at C-Level offers excellent insight and advice to executives on the importance of why they should get more involved to ensure that their teams are strategically aligning, designing, and executing a meeting or event based on the company's goals and objectives. The examples given are based on real-life experiences and offer insight into a perspective, which unfortunately is not the common practice in the way most meetings are looked at today.

After getting to know Eric Rozenberg, sharing our experiences, views, and understanding on the importance and opportunities in regard to face-to-face meetings, I knew that he needed to capture these stories. This is when I suggested that he write this book—as a way to share them as examples with the decision makers.

With my experience of over 20 years on the supplier side and my recent experience on the strategic planning side, I've seen a lot of what Eric speaks about in the book. The "because we do it every year" has always surprised me the most as to the reason why a company holds a meeting, but you would be surprised how often we hear that.

I am certain that after reading this easy-to-follow, charismatic, and informative book, a light bulb will go off, and you will have a different perspective on the importance of bringing your teams, customers, and suppliers face to face, and why strategically aligning them with your goals and objectives will offer you ways to measure and obtain extraordinary results."

Vimari Roman, CMM, CIS
Managing Partner, Swantegy Miami, LLC

"An insightful read—Eric leverages his wealth of experience to walk the reader through a well thought-out process. His stories and personal anecdotes make the process practical for executives responsible for 'face-to-face' investments."

Kevin Olsen
Founding Partner, Keyway, LLC

"The smartest strategy in the world won't help you lead your business if your team doesn't know, understand, and accept it. There's no better medium to getting your critical messages across—whether one-on-one or to groups—than through face-to-face engagement. Nobody knows how to design and execute strategic meetings better than Eric. This book is a must-read for any leader who wants to have a real and lasting impact on the people they work with."

Doron Abrahami
President, River Run Consulting Group, Inc.

"The power of human connection can often be underestimated...until we experience it. Through his stories, Eric weaves a simple yet impactful message to help C-level executives (or any leader for that matter) begin to see the 'Why' of bringing stakeholders together and the importance of aligning face-to-face meetings with their organization's strategy. This is common sense not practiced commonly and makes this book a must read."

Mark Komine
President, WhiteBoard Sales Advisors, LLC,
Former SVP Head of Sales – The Americas
Hilton Worldwide

Meeting at C-Level

An Executive's Guide for Driving Strategy and Helping the Rest of Us Figure Out What the Boss Wants

Eric Rozenberg

CMP, CMM, HOEM, FONSAT

Copyright © 2016, Eric Rozenberg
All Rights Reserved

All rights reserved. No part of this publication may be reproduced, distributed, or transmitted in any form or by any means, including photocopying, recording, or other electronic or mechanical methods, without the prior written permission of the publisher, except in the case of brief quotations embodied in reviews and certain other noncommercial uses permitted by copyright law.

www.ericrozenberg.com

For orders, please send me a message on LinkedIn (www.linkedin.com/in/eric-rozenberg-652199).

ISBN: 978-0-692-73107-9

Dedication

To Elsa—thank you for being always there to support and advise me. I love you.

To Naomi, Shirel, and Tilia—thank you for your patience when I needed to take time to write or when I have to travel. You are the daily rays of sunshine of Mom and Dad's life.

BONUS: REUSABLE PLANNING TEMPLATE

https://swantegy.leadpages.co/35-questions/

Put the lessons from this book into action immediately!

Download the "35 Questions to Align Your F2F Meetings with Your Strategy" and begin planning your next *meeting with meaning* now.

Table of Contents

Introduction

How do you turn moments into momentum? Well, you do that by meeting face-to-face first! ... Don't miss out on the moment that matters most, which is the first meeting.

—James Curleigh,
EVP and President of the Levi's® Brand,
Levi Strauss & Co.

I was meeting with Mike, a successful commercial director in an international company. He had heard about our work through one of his colleagues and had asked me to discuss with him his upcoming sales meeting.

This is a true story, a true dialogue, and only the name has been changed—to protect the innocent!

Me: So, Mike, why are you organizing this sales meeting?

Mike: What do you mean "why"? I guess—because we do it every year!

Mike's response illustrates a major recurring problem in corporate America: corporations spend millions of dollars hiring bright management consultants and mobilizing senior executives' time to develop strategy. However, when an opportunity arises to align and engage employees on the objectives to be reached through a conference or some other type of event— these same intelligent consultants and executives never harness the power of the face-to-face meetings that they are planning. Yes, they spend a lot of time and money on the events, but when asked why they spent so much time and money—they don't have a convincing response: *because that's what they have done every year* ...

In all fairness, senior executives have little or no experience in using face-to-face meetings to increase their organization's business performance. However, I predict they will have an enlightened perspective after reading this book!

My Experience with Face-to-Face Events

For the last twenty years, I have worked with many Fortune 500 companies and have executed hundreds of meetings, events, and conferences in over 50 countries around the world. No two meetings were the same, and none of them ever happened exactly the way it was planned. However, tens of thousands of people and their organizations have been highly impacted through these meetings. Over the years, I have developed a strategic approach to meetings and a simple but very efficient 7-step methodology, which helps corporations and their executives increase their businesses' performances.

This is what this book is all about—sharing the 7-step methodology for strategically planning and executing meetings in order to help executives increase their businesses' performances. I illustrate each of the seven steps with many concrete situations that my team and I have had the opportunity of experiencing. To truly grasp the significance of each of the seven steps, you'll be reading of meetings we executed in multiple continents across the globe (and yes, we've been responsible for meetings located on every continent on the globe, except Antarctica—well, not yet, anyway!). Each of these stories illustrates something important about the particular step of the methodology that we are addressing. Let me add: we have modified the names of individuals and never used the names of the companies, and you'll know why ...

Regardless of the industry, most companies share one or more of the following challenges: aligning people, implementing strategy, motivating staff, transforming learning into behavior, training, energizing sales, creating cohesion, increasing brand awareness or activating it, engaging with and/or retaining customers and increasingly engage on innovation and generating ideas.

My experience is that in the process of working on any of the above challenges, down the road, there is always a face-to-face of some kind—a sales meeting, a product launch, an advisory board, a trade show, a conference, an incentive trip, etc. Will this face-to-face on its own solve the issue at stake? Certainly not! Will the problem be solved without a face-to-face? Certainly not as well!

What's the Value of a Face-to-Face?

Perhaps, you are even questioning if there is any value in bringing people together in a business environment. To answer that essential question, let me share with you some of the findings of the Meetings Mean Business Coalition (MMBC).

MMBC (www.meetingsmeanbusiness.com) is an industry platform that provides tremendous insight about the impact of the events industry on the US economy and about what C-suite executives think about meetings and events in general.

In early 2016, MMBC published a "Business Leaders Survey" that reported the following:

> From October 6–16, 2015, APCO Insight conducted an online quantitative survey among senior executives in mid-sized to large companies on behalf of U.S. Travel. A total of 150 respondents participated in the survey. To participate, all respondents have to be between the ages of 30 and

69 years old and employed full-time in a senior-level position by a for-profit company. Participants represent a wide variety of industries and company departments, including financial services, healthcare, consulting, retail, manufacturing and hospitality.[1]

Some of the key findings of that survey include the following:

"Face-to-face meetings, conferences and events deliver topline growth and bottom line results for C-suite executives in the United States ...

"Nine in ten say meetings improve their ability to close deals (93%), network (90%) and grow professionally (88%) ...

"Ninety-seven percent of executives say that meetings deliver a return on investment. A majority (53%) says they deliver a *great* return ...

"Eighty-six percent believe they help improve the bottom line ...

"Four in five believe they have attended an in-person meeting, conference or event that would not have yielded the same success as one conducted via video or telephone conference ...

"Executives agree that networking (89%), new business opportunities (86%), workforce engagement (80%), training (73%) and staying up-to-date on industry trends (62%) are best accomplished face-to-face ...

"A majority says that team engagement (94%), collaboration (91%), professional development (88%) and productivity (84%) are improved by participation in in-person meetings, conferences and events ...

"When it comes to making investments in their business, executives find face-to-face meetings to be a high priority (82%)—even more than technology (79%) or customer research (66%)."[2]

CEO Perspectives on Meetings

Last but certainly not least, if you still have any doubt, listen to what those leaders have to say about face-to-face meetings:

"Meetings are beyond business. Business is certainly an outcome, but there are so many other things that bringing people together in-person creates that you don't get in any other forum. I think for me, the most important thing is that it builds relationships—and relationships are all about business, trust, building a network and a community. That's why face-to-face meetings can never be replaced or recreated by technology."

—Christine Duffy, President Carnival Cruises (quote from when she was CEO of CLIA, Cruise Lines International Association)

"The real value of meetings is the personal interaction. Meetings are about face-to-face connections, meetings are about people—and you can't email or text a handshake or a feeling."

—Bill Talbert, President and CEO, Miami Convention and Visitors Bureau

"Nothing replaces being in the same room, face to face, breathing the same air and reading and feeling each other's micro-expressions."

—Peter Guber, CEO, Mandalay Entertainment

"Not only does the meetings and events industry bring people together for collaboration in an unsurpassable way, but it creates the additional aspects of professional, business, and societal benefits."

—David DuBois, President, International Association of Exhibitions and Events

"While meetings and events are critically important to the overall success of the travel industry, they've also proven to be key drivers for securing corporate revenues, winning new customers, closing new deals, and developing high-performing talent."

—Michael Massari, Vice President of Meeting Sales and Operations, Caesars Entertainment Corporation

"When a meeting is canceled, who loses besides our team members? The workers who depend on our business. The hospitality industry. Hotel housekeepers. Restaurant servers. The airlines."

—John Stumpf, Chairman, President and CEO, Wells Fargo

Efficacy and Inspiration = Company Growth and Brand Success

Any senior executive should get inspired by the words of Bill McDermott, the CEO of SAP, when he explains in his book *Winners Dream* why he believes in meetings:

> And I still believed that victories should be celebrated. SAP's annual Winners' Circle had become a sought-after event that inspired thousands of our sales professionals to achieve miracles on behalf of the entire organization.[3]

On the launch day of *Winners Dream*, during the IMEX trade show in Las Vegas in October 2015, Bill McDermott was interviewed via videoconference by my business partner Kevin Olsen (founding partner of Keyway, LLC and chairman of the board and founder of One Smooth Stone). You can watch that 5:45-minute interview at this URL: www.youtube.com/watch?v=QZnso8lJBuQ&feature=youtu.be

In the interview,[4] Bill makes the best case about the tremendous value and effectiveness of face-to-face meetings—and he never gives "because we do it every year!" as part of it. Please read these extracts to learn Bill's reasoning.

Kevin Olsen: Now you, you're launching [*Winners Dream*] today, and I know you've been at a variety of media outlets. Why are you here with us? Why are you here at IMEX America?

Bill McDermott: Because I totally believe that the pageantry associated with a great meeting or a great event inspires people to achieve goals and aspirations and dreams they could have never dreamt of in an email or some internal, boring meeting in a conference call. So I always tried to create a movement.

And if you want to double a business, if you want to get buy-in from people, and if you want to move the economy forward, you've gotta think big. I can think of no better way to bring people together and coalesce them around a movement than a great meeting or an unbelievable event that celebrates the pageantry of what leadership is really all about.

But also to add to the learning, you have to have unbelievable keynotes where you're not boring and reciting the company rulebook. You're actually touching on the thought leadership that you think is moving the planet forward.

And then finally, we want to entertain the customer with the best possible entertainment in the world. And yeah, it costs something to entertain people. But what investment could I make that could possibly be better?

Kevin: You know, in our industry [i.e., the meetings and events industry] oftentimes we are categorized as a cost. We're oftentimes the first thing to get cut. And I know, as an industry, we need more executives like yourself to think of the function of meetings and events as an investment. As something that will measure a return and be on the topside of the business equation versus only from a cost standpoint. Can you share with us how you measure the ROI or the effectiveness on the business?

Bill: We look for the brand equity of SAP. It's now one of the top 20 brands in the entire world. So we look for our brand to improve its value every year.

And then I look at my pipeline. We are now generating about 1.3 billion impressions every time we do a Sapphire [company face-to-face meeting]. So what's that worth? We are now adding about two to four billion, depending on the Sapphire event that we run, in new pipeline each time we do a Sapphire.

What would happen if we weren't to do that meeting? Is it an expense, or is it the best growth idea you could possibly come up with as a CEO, to have a world-class meeting and a world-class event that inspires your people, your customers, the media, the financial analysts' community, and inspires your brand? What's going on out there? Wake these CEOs up, people.

* * *

Bill McDermott is one of the best advocates of world-class meetings and events—because they work—and he has been using them in the most efficient and effective ways both when he was at Xerox and today at SAP.

When Howard Schultz re-launched the Starbucks brand, he didn't send a video to 15 thousand employees. He brought them together in a convention center to experience the brand, to network with their colleagues, to learn about customer service, and to develop a sense of belonging and engagement.

When Marc Benioff wants to share the new features of SalesForce with its customers, he doesn't broadcast a webinar. He organizes DreamForce and takes over the entire city of San Francisco. In 2015, he even had to bring a cruise ship to the San Francisco docks as the hotels were full!

When the top tech companies want to showcase their new product or technology, they don't do it exclusively online. They come to a trade show or organize their own huge event to engage with their customers.

When a US president takes the oath during the inauguration ceremony, she or he doesn't do it in the Oval Office with a privileged few. She or he does it live, in front of thousands of people who especially come for the occasion, though they could have watched it in the comfort of their living rooms.

Nothing replaces the unique and exclusive moments you can experience in a true incentive trip. No recognition beats the feeling of being called on stage in front of your peers for your outstanding performance. No conference call allows you to observe the non-verbal signs of the parties with whom you are negotiating. And no Skype conversation has ever ended with a handshake!

This book is for senior executives who care about successfully implementing a strategy, about getting results, and about aligning and engaging with their stakeholders.

It is not about logistics, negotiation with hotels and restaurants, or the dos and don'ts of meeting planning. Although these are essentials parts in a meeting's execution, many books have been written on the subject, so it is not the topic of this book.

This book is about strategy execution, alignment, and engagement. This is about executing your strategy and reaching your company's objectives through a meeting. It is about the "why" of investing in bringing people together.

All the examples mentioned in the book are true and really happened. Only names and industries have been changed. The stories will inspire you, they will give you new ideas for your business, and they will shed a new light on your meetings and how you can use them strategically. You will never approach your corporate meetings and events the same way. The results will make a huge impact on the alignment of your team, on the engagement of your stakeholders, and on your bottom line.

The US Meetings and Events Industry provides more jobs than the automotive industry, represents billions in economic impact, and brings billions in taxes. One meeting's or conference's attendee spends on average three to five times more than a regular visitor to a city. Talk about economic impact!

Meetings mean business. It is not different for corporations. There are billions invested every year in all forms of face-to-face, and it is affecting everyone in your company. Until today, you were not leveraging your face-to-face opportunities with your constituencies, and you were leaving money on the table. How long can you afford to do this? As Einstein remarked, "Insanity is doing the same thing all over again and expecting different results."

I have no doubt that reading this book, full of sound strategy and concrete examples, will impact your business. I would love to hear about your experience and how in the future you are going to approach your company's meetings and events.

Remember—Facetime will never replace face time!

Chapter 1: Understand

"Would you tell me, please, which way I ought to go from here?"
"That depends a good deal on where you want to get to."
"I don't much care where—"
"Then it doesn't matter which way you go."

—from *Alice in Wonderland* by Lewis Carroll

Victor and I had known each other for quite some years. He appreciated that I wasn't afraid to speak my mind, and every time we met at an industry event, we always had animated and enjoyable discussions about business, life in general, and even politics. As the CEO of a very large group listed on the stock exchange, Victor was always looking for or testing new ideas. I was in a business relationship with one of his divisions, and we were attending a reception at the Arts Hotel in Barcelona, Spain.

The room was beautifully decorated with black-and-white photos of well-known musicians, the champagne was excellent, and as we had already tasted so many delicious tapas, none of us had any appetite left for the upcoming dinner! Holding his glass of Dom Perignon with both hands, Victor looked at me, lowering his tone, and started sharing with me a project he wanted to implement the following year with his executive team.

"What do you think of it, Eric?"

"Well, Victor, that sounds like an exciting idea, and your plan of bringing your top people is certainly the way to go. Now, you shared with me earlier your vision about where your company needs to be in five years—and I'm just wondering—how does this new project that you have in mind really align with your vision? Sorry, I just don't see the link."

He stared at me for few seconds without saying a word. I smiled candidly, as I was starting to think that I had missed another opportunity to shut my mouth, when he asked me, "Why is it that nobody in my team is asking me that question?"

"Victor, I guess because I don't care if you fire me! No seriously, I do, but I guess I'm not concerned whether you're going to give me a good evaluation at the end of the year or not, or if speaking my mind will affect my future in your company or not. I'm not in the politics of your organization."

As this true story exemplifies, *understanding* the long-term plan of your organization helps you identify the objectives of a meeting. How does the meeting help you to execute your strategy? What should be the outcomes of the meeting? What are the specific objectives of the meeting?

Clarity around Vision and Strategy

Let's revisit this dialogue from Lewis Carroll's *Alice in Wonderland* that opened this chapter:

> "Would you tell me, please, which way I ought to go from here?"
>
> "That depends a good deal on where you want to get to."
>
> "I don't much care where—"
>
> "Then it doesn't matter which way you go."[5]

As the dialogue above so beautifully demonstrates—it is essential for the success of any organization that everyone *understands* its vision and objectives, and it is crucial that you do so before thinking of organizing any meeting. Each specific face-to-face needs to help in delivering the vision and must have a specific place in sales, marketing, and/or communication strategies. Otherwise, it is a waste of time and resources.

According to author and consultant William Schiemann, only 14 percent of the organizations he polled report that their employees have a good *understanding* of their company's strategy and direction.[6]

This is just unbelievable to me. This means that a vast majority of organizations are missing the point of aligning their constituents, which means that many people are going to work every day without knowing where their organization is going and what their role is in that big picture!

Imagine the impact this is having on employee motivation and on the company or association's bottom line.

This is why it is so important to start planning your meeting with the understanding of your organization's vision and the meeting's objectives. From there, you will target not only the employees but also the vendors and all the stakeholders that have a role to play in the success of the organization and in the delivery of any meeting.

Small or large, internal or external, in the planning process of any meeting, the very first step is to *understand* the organization's strategy. If you don't know where you are going, any advisory board, sales meeting, incentive trip, or customer event will do ... but you might just be throwing your money out the window with little or no impact!

A Way to Establish Clear Positioning

Accordingly, you, as a leader, need to make clear where the specific meeting fits into your overall strategy, what you expect to achieve at the end of the meeting, and where it fits in comparison with all the other touchpoints your organization has with each set of its stakeholders. A concrete and simple way to put this type of planning into practice is to look at it like a matrix, or an excel sheet.

WHO	OBJECTIVES ⟩	YEAR 1				YEAR 2				YEAR 3			
		Q1	Q2	Q3	Q4	Q1	Q2	Q3	Q4	Q1	Q2	Q3	Q4
Staff													
Sales Force													
Customers													
Media													
Shareholders													

On the first line, you indicate the overall objectives of your company for the next three years with specific objectives per quarter.

In the first column, you indicate, one under the other, every stakeholder related to your organization: staff, sales force, customers, media, shareholders, etc.

Then, in front of each stakeholder, in its corresponding line, you write down every regular touchpoint you have with them: weekly calls, annual meetings, monthly webinars, sales meetings, customer appreciation events, incentive trips, etc.

In doing this, you can readily visualize the position of your meeting as you now have a complete matrix in front of you. You can then identify exactly what is expected from this specific face-to-face, where it fits into your marketing, sales, or communication strategy, and what you should be expecting from this particular event in relation to the overall strategy of your organization.

Why is this important?

Because it is going to help you define the specific objectives of the meeting because you will also be able to link it to the other touchpoints you have with a specific line of stakeholders and also with the organization as a whole.

It is important because you will know how to integrate this face-to-face into your marketing and communication strategies and because you will be able to leverage the outcomes of this meeting farther by *understanding* its role and place in the entire process.

Last but definitely not least, it is important because it will give you the opportunity to better define your objectives and key messages for this specific meeting in terms of how it will help your organization in the execution of its strategy and why it is important to invest in the strategy.

Additionally, in using this matrix or spreadsheet, you will know what success looks like for the meeting. You will be able to define its KPIs and how you're going to measure them.

To say it in a simple way: it is important because you will be able to leverage the power of your meeting and instead of spending money without knowing why, you will now invest strategically in your event to increase your business performance!

The majority of the challenges faced by an organization usually revolve around the following: aligning/engaging the team, customers/increasing sales, training/motivation, and culture. I'm fully convinced that without a face-to-face, you will not succeed in solving any of these issues. Having said that, a meeting in itself will never be enough to solve an issue either. Hence, it is important to *understand* the "why" of your event and to build the content around it.

Trickle-Down Alignment: Starting at the Top

Nathalie is a very successful corporate executive. We hadn't seen each other for at least ten years when I entered the business lounge at Brussels Airport and bumped into her at the coffee machine. The serendipity of life has always been my favorite networking opportunity! We started chatting about life, family, and old friends when she asked me what I was up to. I told her about the meetings and events industry, how it was not leveraged by corporate senior management, and the missed opportunities for organizations. Nathalie then proceeded to tell me that she was presently on the board of a large financial institution and that she could very much relate to what I just said. She suggested I meet with her and several of her colleagues from communication and marketing.

Two weeks later, I was in her office with her and seven of her closest colleagues. I started asking questions about their strategy, their goals, their meeting portfolio, and especially about the 10 thousand-person company-wide meeting that was on their radar. I asked about their objectives, what they were trying to accomplish during that event, and what success would look like.

They told me the event's objectives involved sharing a new strategy with employees, explaining the changing environment in which they were operating, and aligning all their employees with the company's objectives. Actually, they all insisted heavily on the alignment part: "We need to align everyone," "We should all be aligned on our objectives," "Success will be achieved through alignment of everyone in the company," and "It's important that we all speak and walk in the same direction."

I paused for a few seconds and then asked, "Can I borrow sixty seconds of your time? Okay. Please take a piece of paper and write down, each of you separately, the three main objectives you believe your financial institution should pursue in the next year."

Then I collected all the answers, compiled them, and shared the feedback, "You have about ten different objectives here in the room with just eight people. You eight are not aligned, and you're expecting to align 10 thousand people. I think you should first start by aligning yourselves."

A few seconds of silence started to convince me that I was about to be kicked out of the room ...

Nathalie looked around the room and finally declared, "I think you just made an excellent point. We need first to align ourselves before looking at our big event. How can you help, and where do we start?"

The big takeaway I want you to gather from this story is—from the moment you have defined your strategy, you should verify that everybody, from board members to the senior executive team, *understands* it and can explain it the same way. This is a simple best practice, which is yet to be implemented by many organizations.

A Compliance Issue: Aligning Around a *Why*

In closing this examination of the importance of *understanding* the strategy of your organization and of asking questions in order to define the "why" of a meeting, I'd like to share with you an amazing story about an innovative advisory board that brought very tangible results to a pharmaceutical company.

Since he graduated from business school, David has been working in the pharmaceutical industry. A very successful executive, his career brought him to different cities in North America and Europe, and he enjoyed an amazing track record in launching or developing different products, including a very well-known pill ... which is not a blue M&M for Smurfs!

We'd known each other for many years, and I had always admired his intellect and thirst for innovation and for challenging the status quo. We were discussing his new position as the pharmaceutical company's worldwide head of a division dealing with a particular chronic disease. To my question "What is your main challenge today?" David immediately answered, "Big issue with compliance."

I know about compliance! I deal with it regularly in business, but I didn't want to assume I knew what it meant for him in his industry, so I asked him to explain precisely what compliance meant in his world.

"Well," he told me, "the general problem in chronic disease is that after six months, between 30 and 50 percent of patients don't take their drugs regularly. It can be because they are fed up, because they think that they have been cured, or because they haven't had any issues lately. Whatever their motivation in their mind is, they decide to stop taking their drugs. That is our compliance issue, and obviously, it has a huge impact on the success of the treatment. By the way, this is not specific to our company or our product, but it is a general statistic across the board for any company dealing with chronic disease."

An idea popped in my mind, so I asked, "David, why don't you do an advisory board?"

He looked at me amused and shared, "Eric, we've been doing advisory boards for twenty years!"

"Yes, but, let me guess—you've probably been doing advisory boards with people from the pharmaceutical industry, reflecting on issues from the pharmaceutical industry, and coming up with solutions for the pharmaceutical industry."

"Go on!" he urged, suddenly puzzled by my comment. "What do you mean?"

"I'm listening to you, and from what you're telling me, this compliance issue, the fact that people are not taking their drugs regularly, it's first of all a personal decision. So instead of having specialists, doctors, and people working in the pharmaceutical industry, why don't you invite somebody from Weight Watchers instead? Or somebody from a loyalty program of an airline, a hotel, or a car rental? Or a behavioral psychologist?"

He loved the idea, and we decided to set up an advisory board exclusively made of people who were not from the pharmaceutical industry and who would have something to do with personal psychology and loyalty.

Understanding his division strategy, we defined together goals for the meeting: at the end of the day, we would need to have at least three new ideas to be implemented.

Then, we defined together a short list of individuals whom we thought were totally suited for what we were trying to achieve. We managed the contract and NDA parts, and David wrote an input paper to set the scene and to explain to each advisor what the challenges were.

After reading the document, I explained to him, "David, I'm sorry, but it's too complicated for non-pharmaceutical people. There is too much information, and a lot of it is not really relevant or necessary for the people on this advisory board to know in order to *understand* your compliance issue." So I helped him by writing the document in a more easy-to-*understand* way for non-pharmaceutical professionals.

Afterwards, we organized a separate call with each advisor, a call with David and another call with me. We wanted to activate each participant's thinking process ... and also check that they had read the input paper and were fully prepared for the full day of face-to-face meeting and discussions.

Finally the day came when we all gathered together. I facilitated this innovative advisory board, and another person took all the notes. The following week, David and I met to debrief everything and evaluate the outcomes.

We ended up with eight action points. Two were rejected by the regulatory department, and six were implemented—and those six had an amazing impact on the compliance issue.

What I hope you gather from this story involves assumptions around *understanding*. Even though I *understood* the notion of "compliance issues," I did not assume that I *understood* David's particular compliance issues, which led me to question him about them. David, on his part, did not assume that because I wasn't a member of his industry that my idea to have an advisory board composed of non-pharmaceutical advisors was a bad or *misunderstood* one. He was open to hearing a different point of view and to looking for innovative approaches in order to solve a major problem—and it worked too!

And that's what I encourage of you: openness. Don't assume you *understand* or assume that someone with a different idea is *misunderstood*. And just as it happened for David, through an innovative and first-ever type of face-to-face event, your business could be massively impacted in a positive direction as well.

BIG Chapter Takeaways

It is essential to *understand* an organization's strategy before even thinking about any type of meeting.

It is equally important to verify that every senior executive and every stakeholder involved in the planning process and the execution of the meeting are on the same page.

The C-level executive responsible for the meeting as well as the meeting planner must *understand* the "why" behind the meeting before embarking upon organizing it. All the participants must also *understand* the "why" in order to participate fully and gain the designated outcomes. Everyone must *understand* the "why" of the meeting.

Next Up

Now that we know the importance of identifying the strategy of an organization, we are moving to phase two of the process: *identify*.

We want to *identify* the various stakeholders: who will be attending the meeting? Who will be impacted by the meeting before, during, or after?

We also want to *identify* the transformation or outcomes expected: why are we investing time, money, and resources in this meeting?

Accordingly, we want to be able to *identify* the objectives of the specific face-to-face: what will success look like, and how will success be measured?

Chapter 2: Identify

You will never see eye-to-eye if you never meet face-to-face.

—Warren Buffet,

Chairman and CEO, Berkshire Hathaway

James was a very prominent professor at a very well-known US business school. He was notorious for his writings and speeches about engagement, motivation, and negotiation. The FMCG company that had hired him was looking forward to getting him in front of their European sales force, which was meeting at Le Meridien in Lisbon, Portugal. James was the highlight of the three-day program and the keynote on the last day, bringing it home for everybody in the room and instigating follow-up actions. Other than the attendees from the UK, none of the 200 people in the room had English as their native language ... and some of my friends would even argue that the UK and the USA are two countries divided by the same language!

James was so good and so busy that he would neither take any preparation call from us nor was he willing to attend the rehearsal the night before. Unfortunately, and despite our insistence, the client didn't want to weigh in on James' decisions on this.

And James got on stage ...

The first ten minutes were really awesome, and James had the attention of the full audience. The translators in the cabins in the back were doing a great job, and his content was indeed excellent. Then, it happened! James paused, looked at everyone, and went on a ride in his speech, "So, you are at the bat. You want to hit the ball hard, very hard so that you can get it out of the park or at least to first or second base. How do you prepare yourself for that?"

"That's it," I thought, "He is out," and indeed he was.

The audience started mumbling, one individual started laughing, and everyone in the room started talking. James lost it and even threatened to stop there and walk out of the room if silence wasn't immediately restored.

This was an epic scene I will never forget. I don't know if anyone ever told him, as of course he didn't want any debriefing, but baseball is NOT played in Europe, and in the United Kingdom, the closest thing that comes to it is cricket. In other words, his comments fell flat because he hadn't *identified* the fact that the audience was not American. And worse, he lost the attention of the entire audience and managed to miss the point he was trying to make!

The Three Elements to Identify

Understanding the strategy of an organization and the why of a meeting, as we have seen in the previous chapter, is the first essential step. Assuming this is done, next you want to be able to *identify* your stakeholders: who is going to attend the meeting? What is their profile? What are their needs? What makes them click? What are their fears? What is the transformation or outcome expected from the meeting?

Accordingly, this chapter is about *identifying* three main elements of your face-to-face event:

1. What are the objectives of the meeting?

2. Who are the attendees and/or various stakeholders involved (as illustrated in the "James example" above)?

3. What does success look like, and how are you going to measure it?

If you want any type of transformation to be executed, it's very important to *understand* where the face-to-face fits in your overall strategy. We have seen "how" in the previous chapter.

Based on the various stakeholders and the different types of face-to-face meetings, you should then be able to work on the specific meeting at hand—what are its objectives? What do you expect from it? How does success look? What should participants be able to do after the meeting? How do you want them to feel?

Digging Deep to Identify the Challenges at Play

Let me share with you two additional examples to illustrate the importance of *identifying* (1) what the organization is trying to achieve through the meeting, (2) what the challenges are that it is facing in setting up the meeting, and (3) who the attendees are.

I met Luc when we organized a sales meeting for the pharmaceutical company he was working for. We received the first briefing call early in December and ended up with 250 people at the Sofitel in Marrakech, Morocco—six weeks later in mid-January! In other words, we spent a large part of our Christmas holidays working together (I've been told that it is now called "winter holidays," but I love traditions!). It was the best sales meeting of the last seven years according to participants' post-event evaluations, and Luc and I developed a great relationship.

When Luc later contacted me, he was working for an international insurance company as its new CMO for about two years and wanted to organize a big kick-off meeting for all the employees with the objective of sharing with them the new strategy that was going to be implemented.

In order to really *understand* the strategy and *identify* its key components, we spent quite some time talking about it—what it meant for the company and the employees, and what they were hoping to achieve. Then we narrowed it down to the goals of the kick-off meeting. Finally, we agreed that I was going to interview some of his colleagues in different departments and at different functions in order to get their perspectives on the new strategy.

In our next meeting, I came back with my findings. I closed the door, sat in front of Luc, looked him in the eyes, and shared, "Luc, I'm afraid most of the people don't care about your new strategy."

"What? Do you expect me to share this with the board? What is going on?"

"You are introducing the Internet in all the processes, and their first and main concern is to know if they are going to keep their jobs—or lose them."

"But we want to keep everyone!"

"OK. So start by telling them that and then, instead of giving them the strategy and asking them to run with it, why don't you help them visualize what their daily work will be when the new strategy is in place?"

This might sound like a detail to you, but it was actually a turning point—even a tipping point—in the organization in terms of the strategy launch and its successful implementation.

Luc bought into it, and we decided that the best way to convey the message to the entire company at once was to—create a theater play with every scene illustrating the life of each department when the new strategy would be in place. We hired a professional scriptwriter and theater coach, and convinced the entire board, mainly introverts, to become actors for one session!

At the end of the presentation, the entire board got a standing ovation because everyone understood they had taken a risk by getting on stage—and more importantly, because everyone understood that they were committed to making the implementation a success.

Last but not least, early in the planning process, department meetings had been scheduled for the week following the kick-off meeting. Each department head met with her or his team and delivered the same message: "You have seen that everyone is keeping their job. You have seen what the life of our department will look like when the new strategy is in place. You have seen where we want to go in two years. Now ... let's work backwards, define the various milestones, and distribute responsibilities among us."

As you might guess, it was a tremendous success.

What I want you to notice from this story is that while Luc could easily *identify* the objectives and the attendees of the meeting—*identifying* the challenges in setting up the meeting proved elusive because these challenges hid underneath assumptions he'd been making. However, because I could work as an outsider to gather employees' perspectives, we were able to uncover and *identify* the challenges at play—the attendees' fears and assumptions about the new strategy. From here we easily designed the meeting so that the attendees could move beyond their initial perspectives to grasp Luc's vision of the new strategy.

More Digging Deep to Identify Hidden Assumptions

The second example I want to share relates to the importance both of *identifying* the objectives of a meeting and also of being able to listen to the stakeholders and *identify* the expected outcomes. In this case, a radical change in stakeholders' attitudes and behavior was needed in order to achieve the meeting's objectives and the company's biggest goals.

Jessica, the European sales director for an international medical devices company, called us to help in the preparation of an important European product launch. The product was hitting number one in the States and was going to help the company to become number one in several European markets.

She told us that she wanted to bring the 120 European top sales people together, to train them about the new product, to train them about the new sales playbook, and to motivate them. She also agreed to let us interview about 25 individuals.

When I came back to her, I shared with her the following.

Eric: Jessica, I have good news and bad news! The good news is that your sales people are very excited about coming for the product launch. The bad news is that I believe you have a bigger problem than getting them together and training them about the new product and sales.

Jessica: What do you mean?

Eric: Your sales force has a mentality of "number two." Every time I ask them questions about their expectations about the sales meeting, they start speaking about your main competitor without me even asking questions about them. And by the way, I learned that your company has been number two for the last seven years. So, if you want to be successful, I believe you should work first on changing their attitudes and behaviors so that they become number one in their minds before anything else.

Jessica understood and agreed, so we helped her prepare the content of the meeting and coached her for her introductory speech—with the first objective—

shift their mindset from number two to number one—in mind.

During the meeting's opening session, Jessica went on stage and started speaking: "Ladies and gentlemen, welcome! We have an amazing program in front of us, and more importantly, we have a new product that is number one in the US because of the following features…. This new product is going to position us as the undisputed leader in all our European markets—but we have a huge problem."

Jessica paused and mentally counted to three while looking at everyone in the room. Not a sound in the room … she'd gotten their attention.

"The problem is that you all sell like a number two! I sell like a number two—and guess what? We have been number two for the last seven years. If we want to be successful and really leverage all the features of our new product, we need first to change our mentality. We need to start selling like a number one!"

The next thing we did will remain in the history of meetings and events as the most expensive setting that's ever been implemented (just joking!). We moved the attendees to the adjacent room where we did something like a gigantic speed dating session. Sixty people on one side played the customers, and sixty people on the other side practiced "selling" the new product to the "customers."

We made them do rotations and take turns in both positions for about two hours. Afterwards everyone returned to the plenary to debrief the experience and explore new ideas. From the practice session, attendees realized that 80 percent of the likely customer objections to the new product were the same, regardless of customer country of origin, and 20 percent of likely customer objections were more nationally or culturally based. In response, they modified their training program per market and created an intranet where all customer objections (including new ones) were posted with the best responses (and the names of the contributors). This intranet of potential customer objections and corresponding responses became the basis for the content of the sales force's weekly meetings.

Needless to say—the outcome of the product launch far exceeded expectations. It was the most successful product launch the company and sales force had had in years! Talk about a mindset shift to number one!

As you see, both from this story and the previous one about Luc, it is very important to *identify* (1) the company's objectives and at the same time to *identify* (2) the stakeholders' concerns, (3) the why of the meeting, and (4) the expected outcomes. Going through these simple but efficient steps will guarantee that you are delivering the right message to the right audience and that your meeting is aligned with your organization's objectives.

The Guiding Template for Accurate Identification

Over the years, we have developed a template of questions that guides us in every project we are involved in. I'm happy to share it with you as it has proven to be very successful, regardless of the industry and the type of face-to-face event. It is divided into eight components.

1. Our Organization

What is our positioning? What is our strategy/our painted picture? What is the competition like? What part of our strategy or of our painted picture do we want to focus on during this meeting?

2. Proposition

What is the key message we are trying to convey? I know it sounds tempting to start adding multiple messages and objectives but the closest to one you go, the more effective your meeting will be, the more focused your content will be, and the more powerful the results will be.

3. The Attendee

Who do we want to convey this message to? What do we know about that person? What are her/his ambitions at work? What are her/his aspirations in life? Do not hesitate to build a fictional profile based on the audience.

4. Emotional Benefits / Insights

What will convince the attendee? What will make them change their behavior? What moves them? What makes them click? What are their fears? How do they generally react and to what?

5. Unique Experience

Where will the experience take place? In which circumstances? What unique experience did attendees enjoy in the past? What worked? What didn't? This can be set from the start or emerge from the creative concept.

6. Definition of Success / Business Objectives

What are the quantifiable results that will determine the success of the meeting? What will success look like? How are you going to measure it? What are the tangible and intangible results expected?

7. Mandatories

What must absolutely be included or absolutely avoided?

8. **Resources and Scope**

> Who should be involved in the project? Who
> has the decision power? What is the timeline?
> What are the deadlines? What is the budget?

Feel free to add your questions (and to share them
with me on LinkedIn–www.linkedin.com/in/eric-
rozenberg-652199).

BIG Chapter Takeaways

Once you've decided to have a meeting, and you
understand the why behind the meeting, then you
must *identify*—the meeting's objective, the
stakeholders (their mindset, reality, or concerns), and
the expected outcomes of the meeting.

Use the guiding template in this *identification* phase
because you don't want any assumptions to cloud your
thinking and throw the success of your meeting (and
the success of your business) off track.

Next Up

You are now ready to get to the heart of the face-to-
face event: *designing* its content.

Chapter 3: Design

I've learned that people will forget what you said, people will forget what you did, but people will never forget how you made them feel.

—Maya Angelou

This is precisely what *design* is all about—content, emotions, and impact.

In the first chapter we explained why it was important to *understand* the strategy and the objectives that the organization wants to pursue in its meeting and how to do it.

In the second chapter, we detailed how to *identify* the various stakeholders and how to *identify* the objectives of a meeting and its expected outcomes.

In this chapter we're going to speak about the *design*. We *understand* why we're doing this meeting. We've *identified* who is attending this meeting, the expected outcomes and the KPIs, and how we're going to measure success. We now have to work on the *design* of the meeting.

The *design* includes several items like the agenda, the learning that people should receive, and the communication they will engage in (before, during and after the face-to-face). The *design*, and in particular, the communication, provides a great opportunity to bring a lot of creativity into the content. It is also where you use technology, not for the sake of using technology but for the purpose of creating something new, something memorable, and something that will really impact people.

Emotion is the most important aspect of the meeting—regardless of whether it is a sales meeting, a product launch, a trade show, or incentive travel. The emotion entails how you are going to make the attendees feel that they are part of something unique and impacting.

And emotion is created through the *design* and the content coming together. To create emotion, here are some important questions to consider: how do you want the participants to feel by the end of the program? What do you want them to remember?

As we all know, creating emotion makes a lasting impression. We've seen in the story of Jessica and her medical device company from the previous chapter that we can create a particular design, for instance, product-launch speed dating. Obviously the design was set to help the organization reach its goal.

Regardless of the type of meeting you are considering, the *design* is really the centerpiece that is going to align everything with your organization's objectives while creating unique and memorable memories for the attendees. One of the best ways to illustrate the importance of the *design* and how it can affect attendees for a long time is to give you some examples about an incentive trip.

Let's first see how effective incentive trips are and then, let's define once and for all, what a real incentive trip is and what you can expect in terms of leveraging the engagement of your participants.

Using Incentive Trips to Explore Excellent Design

In the last twenty years, I have heard many people saying that they have been on incentive trips or many C-level executives mentioning they used incentive trips. In reality, however, these people were just engaging in pleasant group travel, which isn't the same as an incentive trip. Accordingly, these executives were never able to leverage the power of *design* and the power of an incentive trip. I guess you don't know what you don't know ...

As a C-level executive, you want facts to support your opinion and to convince your peers in your executive team. The Incentive Research Foundation (www.theirf.org) provides tons of research and studies about how positively participants respond to incentive trips. Here below are some facts that show the efficacy of non-cash rewards like incentive trips:

- "100% of the Best in Class companies [i.e., those enjoying the greatest customer retention and increase in sales] offered group travel and 100% offered company sponsored events to recognize year-end sales success."[7]

- "Organizations that provide non-cash reward/recognition had an average year over year annual corporate revenue increase of 9.6% versus 3% for all others."[8]

- "74% of US businesses use non-cash rewards to recognize and reward key audiences in the form of incentive travel, merchandise, or gift cards."[9]

- "46% of businesses running non-cash programs include incentive travel as an award, spending $22.5 billion per year."[10]

- Incentive travel is not used exclusively for sales people: 53% of the businesses use it for sales, 43% use it for all their employees, 33% use it with their channel partners, and 27% use it for customer loyalty.[11]

The amount of data available is just amazing and speaks to the fact that most people are appreciative of recognition and that money isn't the only motivator!

There are three elements in an incentive trip. The first element—participants should not be able to put a monetary value on what they are experiencing. Instead of giving away a product, an object, a special evening, or a show, you want to create something different—something that is beyond a mere giveaway. Why? Let me explain by giving you a story.

A few years ago, a media company gave away a flat screen TV to all of its employees. Unfortunately, at the same time the TV was on sale in a large retail store chain, so when employees got home, the comments from their significant others were along these lines: "You see? You work like crazy for this company, and the only reward they are able to give you is this TV, which is on sale at that price!"

Even worse, the following week, several of the employees put their TVs on eBay!

So the first, very important element of an incentive trip is that participants should not be able to put a price on what they are experiencing.

The second defining and essential element is contrast. For example, one night you have a black-tie event at the opera with paparazzi, and the next day everyone is in jeans riding Segways and eating sandwiches for lunch. You want rhythm in your program, you want to keep the attention and the excitement of your attendees, and you want to make the unique moments stand out. You want to play on colors, you want to use music, you want to change rooms during sessions or during a lunch break, change the layout of the room where you are meeting for so many hours. What is important is to create contrast during the program.

The third and most important element that really defines an incentive trip is that participants must experience something unique, something they will be unable to duplicate if they go back to the same place with their friends or families.

It is not enough to host them in a beautiful hotel on a beach, to welcome them with a nice cocktail, to finish the program with a farewell dinner, and in between, let them cook on the beach. This is a waste of your money. This is a waste of your time. This is not leveraging the impact that creating unique emotions can have. This is not an incentive trip. It is a nice group travel program. In an incentive trip, the concept is different, the amount of work involved is different, the budget is different, and the results in terms of engagement and motivation are totally different.

Allow me to make the point and to take you on a journey from Victoria Falls to New York via the Arctic Circle.

Bush-whacking at Victoria Falls

At the time when the music industry was starting to be disrupted by digital downloading, we took one of the industry-leading company's main customers on an incentive trip to Victoria Falls, Zimbabwe. The president and the commercial director were specifically targeting their main distribution customers. They had already defined the objectives and the expected outcomes of the program. Interestingly enough, Doug, the company commercial director, was a former army high-ranking official, and all the clients knew about it. So, we decided to leverage that opportunity ...

Prior to departure, the clients received a list of items and clothes to bring with them. They only knew that the selected hotel was The Elephant Hills, but they didn't know anything about the experience they were going to live out in Africa. To maintain the suspense and mystery, each evening, Doug would tell them what to bring and what to wear the next day, but nobody knew what was going to happen, or what the activities or agenda would be.

On the last evening, Doug stood up and announced, "Ladies and gentleman, tomorrow we're going to have a drop-off. We are going to drop you off with a guide somewhere in the bush. You will need to find clues, answer questions, and find your way back to the hotel. This is going to take you anywhere between an hour and a half for the fastest—or up to two hours and a half for the others. You have an emergency number to call if you need assistance with the clues ... but then you will loose points. As they say in *The Hitchhiker's Guide to the Galaxy*—don't panic!"

The participants were completely stunned. Some even reacted, "Doug, seriously, this is supposed to be an incentive trip! Is this a joke?" He reassured them but, nonetheless, didn't back down from the plan. He then announced the different groups and the different timings when groups would leave the hotel. As crazy as it sounds, the relationship with the clients was so strong that everybody decided to play the game!

The next morning they were all ready to leave. We split them into small groups of five to six. We put them in a jeep, and off we went! When their jeep was out of sight, it stopped and the passengers were asked to get out of the vehicle. A little stressed and wondering what was going to happen, they were very attentive to what Doug was going to say: "Ladies and gentlemen, there is no drop-off! You're not going to walk. Instead—you are about to fly over Victoria Falls." They all screamed because they were going to ride in a helicopter ... and also because they were *not* to be dropped off in the bush and have to make their way back to the hotel!

The point here is that, if you know in advance that you're going to have a helicopter tour over Victoria Falls, from the moment you arrive, you're going to ask yourself, "When is the helicopter tour?" You will be excited but that would be it. There is no leverage in there.

In the example I just gave you, the attendees didn't know about it and were not expecting it—so the moment it came, they were very surprised and felt even more excitement than if it were a planned, expected event in the agenda. The surprise effect was total ... and the extra cost was just in renting a jeep for the whole morning and creating the "drop-off in the bush" scenario.

In this way we leveraged the most emotion and the greatest impact through our *design* of the trip.

An Ice-breaking Event ... Of Sorts

My second example will demonstrate the importance of *designing* a program that is in line with the objectives of the company and *understanding* who the stakeholders are. This incentive trip took place in the Arctic Circle.

Marty was the general manager of an international insurance company's Belgian division. She fully understood the impact of meetings as her company had been leveraging them for years and had enjoyed a constant growth year after year, thanks to their meetings and events portfolio. Marty was always in the field, listening to her employees and customers, and she'd spend hours discussing the *design* of a meeting, whether it was a sales meeting, a customer event, an awards ceremony, or an incentive trip because for Marty, a meeting provided a moment that she could seize to drive her vision for the company.

The year was amazing as about 170 salespeople had exceeded their, already ambitious, sales goals. Marty wanted to celebrate it! She wanted something impactful. She wanted to create emotions, and she wanted it to be short and memorable. We spent many hours discussing each step of the program, especially the speech she was going to deliver on the ice field. Content and timing were everything—as you will quickly understand.

The plane had just taken off from Zaventem, Brussels Airport. It was early in the morning, and for those who were living far from Brussels, it was even earlier! Besides Marty and her executive team, absolutely nobody knew where we were going. The check-in desk only read the name of the company (not the destination), and the private chartered flight wasn't shown on the board. The whole crew had been briefed to be quiet about the destination, and nobody said a word.

As soon as we were airborne, Marty stood up and walked to the front of the plane to speak on the PA, "Ladies and gentlemen, a very good morning to all of you. We just took off from Brussels and will be back late tonight as you have been briefed. In the meantime, I'm delighted to let you know that we are going to spend the day in the Arctic Circle and that we are currently flying to Kemi in Finland!"

The entire plane suddenly burst into screams and laughs, and everybody clapped! It was amazing.

As soon as we landed in Kemi, all the guests were transferred to the snowmobile store, and in less than one hour, they were all geared with warm clothes and ready to go! The cortege of snowmobiles started making its way on the ice field, and each group of six was following a Finnish guide. We drove into magnificent landscapes and arrived at a pristine spot. All around us we were surrounded by snow, only snow—and far away in the distance the buildings of a port were just visible. There was nothing around, except two loudspeakers, which were playing selected tunes.

The snowmobiles were lined up, and people walked towards the music. Three huge circles had been marked on the ground, and the entire group took positions on them. The picture was perfect: Marty was surrounded by her 170 colleagues in three circles, all looking at her. She took the microphone, the music stopped, and she started talking. She had tirelessly rehearsed her speech, thinking about each sentence, pausing to reinforce the key points. She made them laugh, she made them think, and as planned, she respected perfectly the timing.

In the last part of her speech, we started playing "1492: Conquest of Paradise" by Vangelis, and she finished just as the refrain was starting. Imagine that music being played out loud and suddenly, not even 100 yards away, the Finnish icebreaker ship Sampo landed in front of us!

I can assure you that everyone in attendance that day still remembers the moment. And that was the whole point—to celebrate the attendees' great accomplishments in a way that they couldn't really repeat on a vacation on their own.

After boarding Sampo, we split the group in two. One group was served lunch while the other was taken on a tour of the icebreaker ship. We then switched the two groups. The ship then returned everyone to the ice field, and as it was nearing the location of our snowmobiles, a last surprise awaited everyone. As the ship came to a stop, full protecting gear was made available for those who wanted to float in the cold water!

The same night, we were back in Brussels! Unbelievable.

Let's continue our world tour to the city that never sleeps, New York City.

Times Square Rock Star—For One Night Only

Michael was the general manager of a company that had been using incentive trips as a means to grow for more than 25 years. Michael had asked us to build a program in New York. However, first, I wanted to know more about the context, so I started by asking him what were the main challenges his company was facing at that time.

Michael: Eric, listen, we have been doing incentive trips as long as I can remember. Just build something great in New York!

Eric: Michael, you know that I will—and can we take ten minutes and discuss the challenges you're facing right now? What would you specifically expect as outcomes of this program?"

Michael: If you really want to know, I can see two main issues. First, we have people that have been with us for 25 years and have experienced so many different things that they are kind of blasé. On the other hand, we have new sales people who are much younger and have been with us for less than three years, so anything you do will be great for them. Second, we actually have three generations working together and haven't yet found the recipe to make all of them work together well. Having said that, I'm not sure you can work on all those challenges in one program!

I've always love a challenge ...

So this is what I came up with:

We brought the attendees to New York. We did a helicopter tour and a private breakfast at Saks Fifth Avenue with a private fashion show before the store opened. Quite frankly, if you're working in this industry and know the right people, it is not the most difficult activity to organize. We had many activities planned, and the best was yet to come ...

On the morning of the day before the last, we brought the group to SIR, a recording studio near the Meatpacking District. Luck had it that the day before, Lady Gaga had been recording there, and the media had mentioned the place. As the group entered the main studio, the band, made up of musicians selected by Song Division, was playing rock n' roll. Even if you hadn't had a coffee that morning, you were now fully awake!

Michael took the microphone and started introducing the musicians, naming the international star or well-known band each of them had played for. He also mentioned Lady Gaga and paused.

He asked for silence and then announced, "Now we are going to split you into four groups. Each group will be accompanied by one of the musicians and will have its own studio. You have two hours to find the tune to which you are going to sing and to write about your experience in New York the last three days. Good luck!"

We had made sure that each generation was represented in each group and that we also had a good mix of company veterans and newbies. Then each group went into its own studio.

Going from one studio to the other, we could see the different dynamics at play, and thanks to the musicians from Song Division, things were progressing well.

After two hours, we all gathered again in the main studio. The musicians regrouped, shared info, and tuned up to act as the back-up band for each group. Later on, Michael used the musicians' easy regrouping and cohesion during the next sales meeting, saying, "You have seen in New York with the musicians that when you are a professional and play with your team, magic happens!"

Each group had the opportunity to perform in front of their colleagues and be recorded with the support of the entire band. You could see that generations or years of experience at the company were totally forgotten and that they were all "singing their song." It was a memorable moment, and they thought the big event of the trip was over ...

In the evening, we walked out of the W Hotel where we were staying, turned right and right again, and started walking towards the Hard Rock Café Times Square. It was a beautiful evening in Times Square, the temperature was perfect, and, as usual, the streets were packed with thousands of tourists and New Yorkers, making their way to Broadway shows and looking at all the billboards or at the Naked Cowboy and his guitar!

As we were approaching the Hard Rock Café, the billboard on its marquee started flashing the company logo! Everyone became ecstatic and started taking pictures. We entered the Hard Rock Café and went into a private room for dinner. Everyone had the opportunity to stand on the marquee and take pictures of themselves at Times Square like they had never done in the past!

At the end of the dinner, the band came back on stage. One after the other, each group had the privilege of singing with the band. At the end, we invited all the attendees to come on stage and sing together the most entertaining song of all. It was another magic moment, and since then, every time they see the ball falling on New Year's Eve or each time they watch a movie set in New York, they remember, "Once in my life, I sang on the stage of the Hard Rock Café Times Square in New York!"

Afterwards, when Michael and I were debriefing, we reviewed the whole program, the outcomes of his colleagues' mentalities, and the two challenges on which he'd wanted to work: increasing the bonds between the three generations and creating experiences that would excite both veteran and new employees.

As you might guess, his comments to me were extremely positive and, looking at him, I mimicked Colonel John "Hannibal" Smith in the *A-Team* who, at the end of each episode, would pull a cigar out of his mouth and declare, "I love it when a plan comes together!"

BIG Chapter Takeaways

As a C-level executive, it is essential that you spend time on the *design* and the content of your meeting.

As exemplified in the example stories I shared both in this chapter and in previous ones, to maximize the results of your meeting—whether a sales meeting, product launch, training, incentive trip, or advisory board—you must get involved in the *design* phase. This is really how you are going to make the greatest impact.

If you have spent so much time in the strategy-planning phase (and sometimes you've invested so much money in a management consultant), you really should get involved in this particular phase of *design*: sharing your experience about what moves your colleagues, *identifying* meeting objectives and KPIs, and creating the most impactful content that aligns with your organization's strategy.

If you don't, you are like a sports coach who's spent a lot of time training the team but then watches their phone during the entire game. What I mean is that if you don't, you are allowing other, less experienced people to make decisions for you, so the resulting meeting will likely be a waste of everybody's time ... not to mention a waste of money too.

Also, if it is an incentive trip that you are *designing*, remember the three key elements: (1) participants should not be able to put a price on what they are experiencing; (2) participants should experience contrasting moments on the trip; and (3) participants must experience something unique, something they will be unable to duplicate if they return to the same place with their friends or families.

Next Up

Let's move on to the *execution* phase and discuss your role as a leader in making sure that your face-to-face meetings will be *executed* as planned and that you and your company will be able to leverage the meeting's impact to greatly increase your business's performance.

Chapter 4: Execute

They did not know it was impossible, so they did it.

—Mark Twain

If anything can go wrong, it will! Murphy's Law is the most applicable rule when it comes to the *execution* of face-to-face meetings. In twenty years, working in over fifty countries in the world, I have never experienced one single program that was *executed* exactly the way it was planned! There is always something unexpected that will happen.

In this chapter, focused on the *execution* of an event, we will explore outsourcing logistical elements versus keeping everything internal and the value of working with a vendor compared to the fee. Plus, I'm going to share some real "war stories."

I have always been amazed by how much time and money companies invest in the definition of their vision, mission, values, strategy, and objectives, and how little they are ready to invest in the *execution* of those very things in their events and meetings.

Once again, take any challenge of an organization, and down the road, in the various steps to solve it, you will find a face-to-face meeting. However, C-level executives rarely make the time to work on face-to-face meetings and don't want to allocate much budget to them either. More often than not, they leave the responsibility to their personal assistants (who already have thousands of other things to do), to junior partners (who are "forced" to accept and would rather do something else), to young product managers who are already overwhelmed by learning the business, or to procurement departments, which are measured on "how much savings from previous years they negotiated" and which generally buy services the same way they buy products.

In other words, most companies do not leverage the power of face-to-face meetings.

About the Role of Logistics

Logistics are extremely important in conveying the main message of an event or meeting. Imagine that you are planning the event to be outdoors. However, when the day of the event arrives, it's raining or the temperature is too cold or the audio-visual production doesn't deliver, then you're not going to be able to convey your message with the same impact.

For this reason, it is extremely important to work with professionals. Everything is a profession, and logistics, as well, are a very important part of an event or meeting. Even still, professionally *executed* logistics alone are not enough in ensuring a meeting has great impact, as we've seen in the previous chapter.

It's extremely important to *identify* (1) who is going to attend the face-to-face, (2) the objectives of the face-to-face, and (3) how the objectives relate to the organization's strategy—to be able to deliver the perfect logistics.

Basically, in terms of logistics, you have three options: (1) you *execute* the event in-house, (2) you outsource it, or (3) you do a mix of both.

In-house Logistics

For the in-house option, it is extremely important to realize that it is going to cost time. Somebody's got to do the job. When you have *identified* the most adequate person to deliver or coordinate the logistics for your company, you have to realize that this person will have to dedicate a huge amount of time (much, much more than what you would predict) and will be overwhelmed by the project, the changes, and the tasks needed to be accomplished to deliver the project. Accordingly, there is also a cost for the company.

Does that person have the expertise? Does that person have the skills to negotiate contracts with hotels, with audio-visual companies, and with all the other vendors? Does she or he have the local contacts in the destination where you're going? Can that person reach out internally to all C-level executives who need to contribute to the content, and do those executives *understand* the importance of that person's role? Does that person *understand* your business, the meeting's objectives, and how to align both? Beyond these questions, there are many other elements that are essential to the success of your meeting, and you have only one chance to get it right.

Outsourcing the Logistics

If you have challenges in finding the right person internally, the second option is to outsource the management of your meeting. There is obviously a cost attached, but it will be easily compensated by the time and money savings brought to you by your external partner or "vendor" as this external partner is known in the industry. While I could elaborate for many pages on how to select your professional partnering vendor, there are many books and articles about it already, and it is not the purpose of this book. Just shoot me an email if you need more help on this matter.

An Internal-External Partnership

The third option, an external vendor liaising with an internal person, is probably the most effective one. The decision to outsource to a professional vendor doesn't remove the necessity of having a point of contact internally. That internal person ideally should be someone that has decision-making power or is in close contact with someone that does. That internal person should also *understand* the company very well, know the attendees, know the different profiles of the attendees, and be able to guide and liaise with the external vendor. Last but not least, that internal person should *understand* the process described here and be able to brief the external vendor on the *understand, identify,* and *design* parts of the process.

In partnership with the internal point of contact, the vendor will bring added value on multiple levels, especially if you don't have the people with the expertise and knowledge inside. An experienced vendor will also save a lot time and a lot of money in the negotiation process.

For instance, imagine that you're going to book a thousand rooms for the next year, but then three months before the project, you realize that you're only going to need nine hundred rooms. If you haven't negotiated well the attrition cost from the outset, then you're going to end up paying for a hundred empty rooms. Additionally, the vendor to whom you're outsourcing must also have knowledge of anything new happening in the industry, new ways of communicating, new technology, and new locations. That's also the type of expertise you're looking at.

For this partnership to be a success, responsibilities and clear outcomes should be defined, and pricing should be clear from the beginning—and this is in the best interest of your company and your vendor too. As a customer, you recognize the value of what is being organized, not only in terms of the time spent but also of the added value brought to you and your company by partnering with your vendor. In the meantime, your budget has little or no elasticity, so you need to know the scope of your investment! Your vendor should also be happy to work with you and be paid for the added value that they are providing, let alone be profitable to remain in business.

Executing logistics is a process that is increasingly perceived as a commodity, hence the decreased perceived value. Rightly so, you shouldn't be paying the same price for a task that can be *executed* by a junior person as for the full coordination of your project that requires a very senior person. The same can be said for negotiation with the venue or an unbeatable price you have seen for a room on the Internet ... which actually gives you an amazing view of the parking lot and not of the sea. There are tasks that require a seasoned professional.

As previously mentioned, when you put on an event, something unexpected will always happen; there is always an unexpected occurrence that changes the plan. In those situations, you need a vendor who can deal with stress, who can find solutions, and who can tap into a local, national, or international network to provide the solution. The main challenge is that many people in charge of buying services apply the same reasoning when buying commodities. You don't buy services like you buy racks of toilet paper! If you do, then expect a s@!# service!

The last point about an outsourcing partnership is related to the fees. There are different ways you could be looking at the fees, so you should basically decide which one is the most appropriate for you and your organization. Some vendors charge a flat fee. Others charge a flat fee and a success fee based on the KPIs you both agreed on from the beginning (which entails your deciding how to measure those KPIs). For instance, finding the proper venue for your program, the ideal hotel that will match all your requirements— that is a profession in itself as well. As it turns out, the venue is a make-or-break success factor in the *execution* of a meeting.

What most people don't realize is the cost structure. People outside the events and hospitality industry will not be able to find a better deal by making arrangements themselves using Internet searches. They will waste a lot of time and will likely end up with a worse deal. So once again, without incurring extra costs you might want to consider getting some help!

The most important part of making an internal-external partnership is that everything is clear from the beginning and that both parties are happy.

That reminds me of the story of the patient suffering from an issue that no other doctor could help her with. So she decided to try another doctor, a very experienced and respected doctor. After ten minutes of consultation, the doctor shared her diagnosis and advice. The patient then enquired about the cost of the appointment. After being told the amount, the patient complained about the price, mentioning that it only took the doctor ten minutes and that it was really overpriced for just ten minutes. At that stage, the doctor looked at her and replied, "I'm not charging you for ten minutes of my time. I'm charging you for thirty years of experience and the ability to give you sound advice in ten minutes instead of hours."

The Insight of External Vendors

There was a US company that was organizing a European conference in Budapest. They had about six thousand attendees. They had a lot of people internally who were working on the conference: some were in charge of the content for the plenaries, some were in charge of the working groups, and others were in charge of the store where they were selling their products. There were many different groups involved internally, and the company had signed a contract with the exhibition center two years before. Things were starting to heat up, and we were called to help them organize it.

The first thing we did was look at the contract they had negotiated with the venue. After careful analysis, *understanding* the company's strategy and the conference's objectives, we came back to them with "interesting" news: "You know what, for the program you're telling us you want to organize, you're going to be missing one exhibition hall for your trade show and at least a day for each of the three exhibition halls you need to realize your project. Somebody forgot that setting up and dismantling will take more than two hours! This was not taken into consideration when you signed the contract two years ago."

We went back to the venue on their behalf and started the negotiation again. Luckily we were able to secure the space for the number of days needed.

The second thing is that we helped them build a budget. When finally the whole budget was put together and all the different groups in the company were asked to align some figures, we consolidated everything and came back to the chief marketing officer with additional "interesting" news: "If the company continues as they are going, they will be more than 30 percent over their budget."

This is just to illustrate the point that again, everything is a profession. It's great to have people internally, but it's also an opportunity to outsource to a professional vendor who knows the craft of putting meetings together.

There are a lot of war stories in my industry, which is also what makes it so exciting to work in. I'm sure one day a psychology student will write a thesis on people like me, people who enjoy finding solutions when something unexpected shows up!

Got Stress?

According to CareerCast (www.careercast.com), the most stressful jobs are:[12]

1. Enlisted military personnel

2. Firefighter

3. Airline pilot

4. Police officer

5. Event coordinator

6. Public relations executive

7. Corporate executive (senior)

8. Broadcaster

9. Newspaper reporter

10. Taxi driver

In other words, it is less stressful to be a corporate senior executive than to be an event coordinator!

If you have a "war story," please share it with me in a few lines through LinkedIn (www.linkedin.com/in/eric-rozenberg-652199). I'd love to hear from you. We can see how it compares with the three true stories that I'm going to share below, all of which illustrate the crucial phase of *execution*.

War Story 1—Locked In, Locked Out— and Ready

"Hurricane Jeanne was the deadliest hurricane in the 2004 Atlantic hurricane season. It was the tenth named storm, the seventh hurricane, and the fifth major hurricane of the season, as well as the third hurricane and fourth named storm of the season to make landfall in Florida."[13]

On September 25th, Hurricane Jeanne was a category 3 and was approaching Florida. I was in Miami at the Ritz-Carlton South Beach, working on a project with a little over a hundred clients from several European countries, who had been invited by a manufacturing company. Ken was the European events director. We had been working with each other for about nine years and enjoyed a mutual trust.

The attendees were in Miami for four days of training before attending a trade show in Washington. After several days of serious work, the last evening on

Friday night promised to be spectacular with a dinner planned in a private house on one of the beautiful islands between Brickell and South Beach—as well as a lot of surprises.

I had been monitoring the weather forecast since we'd arrived, and everyone I was speaking with was very optimistic, "Oh, yeah, it's going to go north. Oh, it's going to go north. Oh, it's going to go north," ... but it kept going west—and was going to hit southern Florida on Saturday night if nothing changed.

As I'd been liaising regularly with my friends at the Miami Convention and Visitors Bureau, I had a very accurate understanding of the weather situation. Late Wednesday night, I had a meeting with Ken.

Eric: We can't stay until Sunday. We need to evacuate on Saturday.

Ken: Are you serious? There is not even a recommended evacuation, let alone a mandatory evacuation!

Eric: I know, but if nothing changes in the trajectory of Hurricane Jeanne, an evacuation is likely to be announced tomorrow night or Friday morning.

Ken: What if we are wrong?

Eric: Do you want to take the risk of having your guests staying in public shelters? I certainly don't— and you can always blame it on me!

Ken: How about THE Friday night event? Is it still going to happen?

Eric: Yep, and it will be unforgettable!

The next morning, I announced the plan to all the participants and told them that they were free to stay, especially those scheduled to leave the coming Monday, but there was a risk that they would need to stay at least one night in public shelters. We started rebooking, actually advance booking, from Sunday to Saturday morning those who were willing to leave early.

On Friday morning, a mandatory evacuation was announced (just as I'd predicted!).

I had a meeting with Franz, the general manager, a seasoned professional, who had been called out of retirement to run the transition at the hotel and who had seen many things in his life. I told him that all the attendees were from Europe and had no family to go to. I came to an agreement with him: those willing to stay would be locked in the hotel and would sign a disclaimer, but those checking out, because of the mandatory evacuation, would not be allowed to return and check back in because it was illegal for a hotel to take in new guests during an evacuation.

On Friday night, as all the guests walked out of the hotel on Collins Avenue, they were greeted by a cortege of six Stretch Hummers, each seating up to 19 people. When everyone was situated in the vehicles, the Miami Police Bikers arrived, in full gear and sirens, and escorted us to the private villa. The night was beautiful—no wind, no clouds, shining stars, a Cuban-themed evening—it was unreal.

The next morning, about sixty percent of the attendees had been rebooked and were leaving the hotel. Around 10 am, the clouds appeared and the wind started blowing while all the Ritz-Carlton employees were fixing the hurricane shields on all the windows around the lobby. Around noon, a group of four attendees who, against our advice, had checked out and tried to buy tickets at Miami Airport were back and wanted to stay in the hotel. They were extremely vocal. I turned them down explaining to them that this was not Europe and that I wasn't going to jeopardize the hotel's license or the opportunity for the remaining 40 attendees to overnight in the hotel as it was totally illegal to take these four, who had checked out, back in the hotel. I found them a great room in the Keys, and they had a blast!

At 3 pm, Franz inserted his keys in the main door locker and locked us in. We were ready for Hurricane Jeanne. In the evening, the main ballroom, which is central in the hotel and a safe location, had been transformed into a dining room, and together with some other clients and the remaining staff, we had a very interesting dinner, exchanging experiences about hurricanes.

Even in those circumstances, the "Ladies and Gentlemen of the Ritz-Carlton" were there to serve! One or two people had to be reassured, but the rest of us, although a little bit nervous, had somewhat of an interesting evening. I went back to my room and watched what was happening outside. There were very strong winds and rain, but we actually had the tail of the hurricane. It was my first hurricane experience, and there are worst places than the Ritz-Carlton South Beach to experience it!

Needless to say that this experience strengthened even further our relationship with the client and the trust he has in our services and our network!

War Story 2—How Many Catastrophes Can You Handle in a Week?

My second story relates to the launch of a revolutionary product for a medical devices company. The product was a game changer and would position the company in first place. No date could be set until production was 100 percent certain that they could deliver on time in order for the sales team to go on the field.

As soon as production gave us the green light, we had two and a half months to put the conference together. Kathleen, their events director, was used to such tight deadlines, and from past experiences, she knew we could deliver. The venue selected was in the south of Sardinia, and as soon as we arrived for the inspection, we had a taste of the level of service we would get when the commercial director of the property answered one of our requests by stating, "But Eric, it is already a reward for your clients to be able to come here." It was not going to be an easy one ...

Because of time constraints and availability of properties capable of welcoming such a large group in only two months time, we had little or no other options, so we had to make the best of it.

We arrived on site on a Thursday. The truck with all the production coming from Belgium was scheduled to arrive the next day by ferry from Italy. We had two and a half days to set up everything in order to be ready for the Monday afternoon rehearsals.

The next day at noon, the driver called, explaining that the ferry captain had just informed everyone that they were having trouble with the engine and that departure would be delayed for a few hours. So far so good—we had a lot of buffer time, so we started to look at other options in terms of transport and material.

Friday late afternoon, the driver called again—there were still no signs of departure. At that moment, I asked him to leave the boat and drive two hours north where he could board another ferry. "I can't" he responded, "I was the first vehicle to move in, and I don't know how many vehicles are blocking me." I instantly went from DEFCON 5 to DEFCON 3 and started evaluating all options, discussing with Kathleen the timing and costs for various other options, including transporting back-up material by small boats or helicopters.

The night was short and in the morning, the driver had positive news from the captain in terms of the ferry departure on Saturday late afternoon—but at that stage, we didn't have much trust in the captain! Finally, as we were about to confirm the ordering of back-up material, the driver called—apparently the boat was moving ... but it would be arriving in the north of Sardinia on Sunday afternoon. Then it hit me: trucks are not allowed to drive in Sardinia on Sunday between 8 am and 10 pm. Moreover, the truck would need to cross four different "Carabinieri" (Italian police) jurisdictions.

"Never give up," they say ...

At that moment, I remembered that Alan, a friend in Milan, had told me that his new son-in-law was a high-ranking officer in the Carabinieri. I called him and while the boat was sailing to Sardinia, we managed to get the four authorizations.

I have never been so happy in my life to see a truck driver! It was midnight, and he just arrived at the entrance of the hotel. We had hired twenty extra people to help with unloading the material and assembling everything. We worked all night nonstop until the next day. By 1 pm on Monday, we were ready for rehearsals. It's amazing what a highly motivated team can do when it works together on a deadline!

Every day was bringing its lot of unexpected changes. Every morning, I was waking up and wondering what crazy thing would happen in the following hours. And one night, we even saved a life!

On the last evening of the program, we were going to show a movie summarizing the highlights of the week. It was 3 am the night before, and we were editing the movie. I was with the editing team, supporting them and giving some input on the final cut so that the last day, we would just need to edit the final activities and award ceremony.

I decided to go downstairs to get drinks for the team. I went down and as the elevator door opened, I saw in front of me a group of people who were surrounding somebody bleeding from the head. I approached the group. Apparently it was an attendee from another group, and nobody seemed to be able to make decision. I spotted my client's UK general manager whom I knew had a nursing background.

"Samme," I asked, "what's going on?"

"The guy was apparently drunk," she replied. "He fell on the back of his head on the corner of a table, and he is bleeding. If the artery was hurt, he might have a few hours or just an hour in front of him. If we press too much, then we might push the bone into the brain, which is obviously not the right thing to do."

I turned to the hotel receptionist and ordered him to call an ambulance. His answer still resonates in my head, "No sir, we have a procedure. If anything happens, we first must call a car, which will take a person to a doctor who will decide if we need to send the patient to the ER."

"You can't fix stupid!" I thought. I took my phone and called Kaï, our local partner, asking him to call an ambulance immediately and to send it to the hotel. Sixty seconds later, Kaï confirmed that the ambulance was coming from Calgari and would arrive at the hotel in 20 to 30 minutes.

How long is 20 minutes when your head is bleeding? I went back to Samme, "Can we move him?"

"Yes," she affirmed, "he can move, but we need to get him to the hospital as soon as possible." We took a minivan, seated the guy inside, and started to drive. I called Kaï back.

Eric: Kaï, we just left the hotel with the guy.

Kaï: Don't move him. You don't know if he can move.

Eric: Kaï, listen to me please. I'm with someone who has a nursing background, and I have already made the decision. We are on our way. Please call the hospital and tell them to get in touch with the ambulance driver. They need to let him know that on the road, he will come across a minivan that will be flashing big lights. It will be us with the person who needs emergency treatment.

That's what we did. We saw the ambulance from afar, started flashing the lights, stopped in the middle of the road, transferred the wounded person into the ambulance, and literally saved his life.

The story finishes well as the next evening, the guy was back at the bar with a huge bandage on his head and a glass of beer in his hand. Go figure!

The whole thing took about 45 minutes, and when I returned to the room of people editing the movie, I was greeted by: "What took you so long? We thought you were going down to bring us drinks."

I responded, "That's right, and I thought that, as I was already downstairs, I could save a life in the meantime. How is the editing going?"

On the last night, as we were celebrating the conference's success, the CEO approached us and looked at Kathleen, "This was an easy one for you this time, right?"

She looked at me, turned back to him, and replied, "Yep, quite easy I must say!"

Once again, this true story strongly exemplifies the power of a strong network and the added-value external professionals can bring, in partnership with an internal decision maker, to an organization.

War Story 3—Never Underestimate the Power of a Volcano!

My third story exemplifies the importance of working with excellent local partners. These are found after years of research, testing, networking at trade shows, and experience sharing with colleagues. They are the backbone of a successful program. They might not always be the biggest names around, but they are certainly the best in the field and give you the greatest value for your money.

Friday April 16, 2010. I was having lunch with some friends in an Italian restaurant in Brussels. When you do lunch in Europe, it is usually acceptable to have one glass of wine ... especially if you are eating the best pasta in town! Marc, a private pilot, declined the great Montepulciano as he was flying a few hours later. Suddenly, his iPhone rang. He spoke for two minutes, hung up, and told me, "On second thought, I think I'm going to indulge in that famous Montepulciano."

Puzzled, I looked at him, then I looked outside at the clear blue sky, and then I looked at him again.

Eric: You're not flying?

Marc: Nope! They just closed Zaventem—Brussels International Airport.

Eric: What? But the sky is beautiful, and there is no wind!

Marc: Correct, but there is the ash cloud from the Volcano Eyjafjallajokull, which is arriving from Iceland, and they are closing the European airspace, one country at the time!

Now imagine for a second that you are attending a workshop on risk management and that someone proposes the possibility that an Icelandic volcano is erupting and that most of the European airspace will be shut down for several days. Wouldn't you think that this scenario was just a little over the top? Well, obviously it wasn't! People were stuck on both sides of the pond.

After several days, some competitive companies jointly chartered flights to bring back their executives from California or New York via Montreal and then Portugal or the south of Spain. As crazy as the scenario was, it was happening before our eyes.

It was Friday afternoon, the airports were closing, nobody knew for how long, nobody knew where the ash cloud was going—and we had five world conferences the following week, including an incentive trip to Vietnam leaving from Paris Charles de Gaulle the following Wednesday.

One hour later, my team was in an emergency meeting. We had called each of the five clients to inform them of the situation and were going to report back, with scenarios and action plans, by the end of the afternoon.

The whole weekend, we worked on these scenarios, rebooking what could be rebooked, looking for what could be done to save each event, looking at where participants were coming from and which programs would be potentially impacted and at which levels.

On Sunday night, none of the airports had yet reopened.

On Monday morning, as I was driving to a client whose event was happening two days later with 120 winners leaving for an incentive travel to Vietnam, Paris Charles de Gaulle was still closed and not scheduled to reopen before, at least, Wednesday, their departure day. We had been in touch several times per day since Friday, and before seeing the client, I decided to call one more time my local partner in Vietnam, George Ehrlich-Adam from Exotissimo (now Exotravel), to share with him my thoughts.

"George, Paris Charles de Gaulle is still closed. It might reopen on Wednesday or not. Even if it does, it is going to be a mess. This is supposed to be a reward and a unique experience for these people. Instead, it is going to be a stressful journey, and these people will be scared that they'll get stuck in Vietnam as nobody has any clue about where the ash cloud is going. I'm on my way to see the client, and my recommendation is that they postpone this trip for two months and do it in June ... at no cost! Are you with me?"

Over the years, through many projects and trade shows, George and I have developed a strong business relationship, and we trusted each other. He was one of the bosses in his company, and he knew I was acting in the best interests of the client, and we shared the same values. He almost immediately replied, "I'm in! Go for it."

Fifteen minutes later, I was in the boardroom with the company's CEO, the general manager, and the commercial director. I'd always enjoyed working with them and especially with Elie, the general manager, who was a true leader that understood very well his employees, knew how to motivate them, and never hesitated to take risks.

Elie: So what do we do?

Eric: We move it to June. We don't know if Charles de Gaulle is going to reopen in two days. If it does, it will be a mess, and your people will be scared that they'll end up stuck in Vietnam because we don't know what is going to happen with the ash cloud.

Elie: What will be the cost?

Eric: For the airlines, the maximum will be the difference between what we paid for a ticket a year ago and the price of the new ticket because Vietnam Airlines has confirmed by email that they are willing to reimburse if we cancel today or to reissue at no costs if we postpone until June.

Elie: And for the land arrangement?

Eric: Nothing!

The three of them together: What?

Eric: Nothing!

Elie: And the Intercontinental in Hanoï?

Eric: Nothing!

Elie: And the cruise and the gala dinner in the grotto in Halong Bay?

Eric: Nothing! I just spoke with George whom you met during the inspection. He understands the situation, and although he is definitely not responsible for it and could charge us 100 percent, he is willing to postpone everything—at no cost.

They couldn't believe what they were hearing. The decision to postpone was quickly taken, and new dates were set for June. I helped them communicate with all the 120 winners. Some immediately called ... to thank the management for indeed, they'd been afraid to leave and afraid of getting stuck in Vietnam! The whole program ended up taking place in June and was a memorable one.

You might wonder if, either between George and us or between the client company and us, there was at least one email sent during the postponing process. The answer is—no! It was such a quick decision that all of to trust each other—only verbal ...tions.

Of course, afterwards, everything was confirmed in writing, but as it was happening, we had to make the right decision together and act upon it in a matter of minutes with only phone calls between us. This might not be possible everywhere in the world.

Once again, the experience and network saved the day, transforming a difficult situation into a positive outcome. For the record, this is the only time in the book where the name George is the real one—and it is the least I can do, with his approval, to recognize him and his agency.

BIG Chapter Takeaways

Anybody who has ever organized anything has experienced very difficult moments, perhaps similar to the ones I described in the stories I've shared in this chapter. Your role as a C-level executive is to select the right partner, to surround yourself with the right people, to be available when important decisions need to be made, especially when it comes to content and finances—and then to concentrate on your own business!

You need to be briefed regularly on the advancement of the project, but you should certainly not be dragged into the minutia of running the logistics. During the program itself, you need to be able to concentrate 150 percent of your time and attention on the attendees, whether they are employees, vendors, or customers. This is why you determine the overall direction of the plan and then commission your internal and external team to *execute* it.

And remember, even though working with an external professional certainly means you are spending money to pay them, the value of that partnership is priceless. Because of vendors' vast experience organizing events and meetings, their connections with venues and service providers, their abilities to work well when faced with difficult, unexpected challenges, and their many partnerships with locals, you will likely save lots of money and time by partnering with them. Plus, you have a much greater guarantee that your event will be unique, memorable, and full of impact both for the morale and the bottom line of your company—which is the whole point of having a face-to-face in the first place!

Next Up

When all is said and done, it's time to move on to the next phase of the process: *measure*. If you don't *measure*, you don't exist, and my bet is that today, more than ever, you need to justify to your colleagues in the executive and/or management team the investment made in the face-to-face meeting. This is what we are going to address in the next chapter.

Chapter 5: Measure

And I still believed that victories should be celebrated. SAP's annual Winners' Circle had become a sought-after event that inspired thousands of our sales professionals to achieve miracles on behalf of the entire organization.

—from *Winners Dream* by Bill McDermott,
CEO of SAP

Georges was the CEO of a bank focusing on businesses and entrepreneurs. Over the years, he had managed to position his company in such a way that, when considering a financial institution for their business, entrepreneurs would always shortlist his company.

It was a beautiful day in September, just after Labor Day, and Georges was sharing with me the plan he was about to launch and the three main strategic imperatives he wanted to focus all his employees on for the following year. Three months later, in early December, he was going to gather his top 100 people at a sales meeting with the specific purpose of

e whole year and preparing for the next
ing to be a very important event.

The discussion quickly turned to ROI and how to *measure* the impact of this meeting.

Georges: Eric, I know you are passionate about *measuring* the impact of meetings, but what about this one? I can certainly *measure* the ROI of any investment or the marketing efforts we are investing in, but what would you *measure* and how would you *measure* it, regarding my December meeting? I'm going to share with the attendees the plan and the priorities for next year, and of course, we will see at the end of next year if we were successful, but how can we even think of *measuring* anything specific in regard to this meeting?

Eric: Georges, I can demonstrate to you that from the moment you have *identified* the objectives of the meeting, you can determine KPIs and *measure* them. They might be tangible or intangible, and there is a lot of theory about it, but this is not the point here ... and you don't have time! Let's focus on your December meeting. You told me that you are gathering your top 100, right?

Georges: Yes.

Eric: You also told me that you have a new plan and three strategic imperatives for next year?

Georges: Correct.

Eric: And I presume that it is essential for your message to percolate to the front-line people facing your clients that your top 100 are fully aware of and aligned with your three strategic imperatives?

Georges: Absolutely.

Eric: OK. Let's say then that one month before the meeting, we determine how many of your top 100 know precisely about your three strategic imperatives. With technology, it's quick and cheap to do. And let's say that 60 percent of them answer in the affirmative.

Georges: Oh! That would be magnificent, but I'm not that optimistic!

Eric: Just for the sake of the discussion, let's assume that you are already at 60 percent. That means that you know a month in advance that you will need to allocate time in the agenda to work specifically on your three strategic imperatives and to bring them from 60 to 80 percent. You will *measure* just after the meeting, and you will *measure* again three months later where these 100 are at. Last but not least, every time you communicate with them after the meeting, you will make sure to remind them of the three objectives, by inserting three key words under your signature, for instance.

Georges: Got it. Makes sense. Let me call my CMO to continue the conversation.

And that's how we started working together ...

This true example illustrates perfectly what you can be *measuring* and also the impact a specific meeting can have on the *execution* of your corporate strategy. It is not always the "full ROI," but there is always something impacting the business and/or bottom line, like in 2000 when we were the first ones in Belgium (and probably in Europe) to *measure* the impact of an incentive travel campaign. The case study was based on programs run for one of the major companies in the music industry. And I will close this chapter by giving you more information on what we did in that program and the conclusions.

My Path to Including "Measure" in the Methodology

In 2005, I finally found a course with scientific background that addressed *measuring* the impact of meetings. Also, I attended Jack Phillips' ROI Workshop in Miami. I went through the entire training program with Jack. He is the founder of the ROI Institute[14] and really brings his education and training *measurement* background to the meetings and events industry. We spent hours discussing. Jack loves to be challenged, so we did challenge him. My conclusion: this guy is good, very good, and his methodology is very strong.

After taking Jack's course, I returned to the old continent (Europe) and started reaching out to all our clients, and I kept smashing my head on the wall until

I finally got the point! Yes, you can *measure* any type of meeting, I'm fully convinced of it, and any time you want to talk about it, as Leonard Cohen would sing, "I'm your man!"

What I didn't understand is that if you are a large company like Salesforce.com with DreamForce[15] or SAP with Sapphire Now,[16] it makes all the sense to *measure* the impact on the full ROI that results from a meeting. Why? Because of the size of your investment, because of the strategic role the face-to-face meeting plays in your sales results, and because you have the system in place and the resources needed to *measure* it.

However, you are not going to *measure* the full ROI of every single face-to-face meeting. In Europe, there is hardly any corporate meeting of that great size. So, each time, I would suggest an ROI *measurement* to my European clients, I would be greeted with high enthusiasm ... until we would estimate the cost of the whole process!

Bottom line: I failed miserably and never found one client willing to invest in a full ROI survey as it takes a lot of time, a lot of resources, a lot of money, and it was too early ... but I still had in mind the universal rule: if you don't *measure*, you don't exist!

I went back to the drawing table and restarted the whole process. The only difference this time was that I followed the methodology described in this book.

Understand – Identify – Design – Execute – Measure – Follow Up – and Uniquely Different ... and it worked!

From the moment you follow these steps, you necessarily find yourself defining (*understanding* and *identifying*) the "why" of the meeting and the KPIs. You can, therefore, always *measure* something. It can be tangible or intangible (as illustrated below in the India example), but from the moment there is a reason, a purpose, and an objective "why" in regard to the meeting, you can and should *measure* it against your objective. It will help you justify the investment, and equally important, it will impact your future decisions about your strategy's *execution*.

As a corporate executive, the most important questions to ask yourself about a meeting are: What do I want to *measure*? How am I going to *measure* it? When will I *measure* it?

A Smooth Landing

Isabelle, a partner in an international service firm, was in charge of the annual meeting we were organizing for them. We had agreed that part of our fee was going to be a success fee based on specific satisfaction objectives from the attendees. We wanted to have at least 80 percent of people answering the questionnaire. Yes, you read me correctly—eighty percent.

The annual meeting was taking place abroad, and we had chartered two planes. On our way back, Isabelle, in my plane, and one of her colleagues, in the other plane, took the PA and asked everyone to take ten minutes of their time to fill in the short survey we had prepared. She explained the reasons, and we just had to collect the questionnaire before they deplaned the flight.

What we did was simple: we *understood* the strategy and the objective of the organization. We *identified* the stakeholders, what the company expected from the meeting, the KPIs, and how we were going to *measure* them. Then we *designed* the content and *executed* the meeting. Afterwards we *measured* against the KPIs on an agreed basis at a time that would give us a significant amount of answers.

The cherry on the cake was that we even simplified the whole planning process for the following years based on the results because we were able to lower the number of internal people in the organizing committee by reporting directly to one of the directors who had decision-making power. It was a true win-win.

On an Elephant's Back

Finally, and as promised at the beginning of this chapter, let me share with you the first study we did in which we *measured* the impact of an incentive campaign. First, I will share how we solved a strategically important sales problem for the client company and how this intangible issue was *measured*. Then I will detail the principles that we developed from what we learned in regard to this incentive impact study.

Ethan was the Benelux president for a major company in the music industry. Back in 1998, we organized an amazing incentive trip for his top clients. It was so successful that when the attendees returned, they jointly bought an advertising page in the middle of the industry magazine to thank Ethan and his colleagues.

Two years later, the music industry was starting to be disrupted by MP3 downloads and was loosing huge market shares for many reasons—but not the least because customers, and especially young customers, were saving their money by downloading music, all the while shifting their spending to cellphones and monthly subscriptions.

To add complexity to the situation, the new Benelux commercial director was not really accepted by the company's main client, a large chain of record stores, whose CEO, a guy named Jaap, even went on strike one day, refusing to buy from them any records for 24 hours. This was a lot of lost revenues for my client ...

The incentive program was scheduled three months after Jaap's strike, and Jaap hadn't yet confirmed his participation.

Ethan personally called him and diplomatically appeased the tension momentarily while getting his commitment to join the incentive trip to India. In the conversation, when Ethan learned that Jaap loved elephants, he promised Jaap that he would get his own elephant!

Three months later, we landed in Delhi. After a quick shower at our hotel, The Taj Palace, we found ourselves on rickshaws in the middle of the Old Delhi Bazaar. You couldn't dream of better contrast! The whole program was absolutely amazing. Our guide, Kalpana, was just out of this world. Her knowledge of India on all aspects was second to none. She was well regarded as her father had been a close friend of the Mahatma Gandhi. We couldn't stop asking her questions and would spend hours, even a whole night, talking. We were nicknamed "The Conversation Club"!

When we arrived in Jaïpur, we visited the "Pink City" and its palace. We were shown through the private door exclusively reserved for the Maharaja. The next day, our coach stopped in front of the Maharaja's entrance door, and as some of the participants were already teasing the driver by telling him that he was taking the wrong path, the huge gate opened!

We were welcomed by the Maharaja himself and enjoyed an amazing lunch with him on the Lalique table of his private room, with pictures of celebrities on the buffet cabinet, including a picture of Prince Charles and Lady Diana ... Magic, it was just magic.

As we drove back to our hotel, Taj Rambagh Palace, the bus stopped at the entrance of the property. A procession was waiting for us with horses, camels, elephants, music, flowers, etc. Ethan approached Jaap and invited him to sit on an elephant, behind the elephant driver. A small note was waiting for Jaap on the back of the elephant:

> Dear Jaap, I know our business relationship has not always been perfect, but I'm glad that you are here with us in magical India and that we've had the chance to experience these moments together. I always keep my promises, and this is your elephant, reserved exclusively for you! Thank you for being here. Ethan.

I was observing Jaap and could see him looking at Patrick with a huge smile and watery eyes.

Later, when I debriefed with Ethan, he confirmed to me that in his business relationship with Jaap, there was a "before India" and an "after India." Could that be precisely *measured*? Of course not—it is the essence of an intangible *measure*. Could it be *measured* without honest feedback from Ethan? Obviously not. Did it have any impact on the business? You bet it did.

Of course, this will never replace the fact that the artists represented by this major company would produce great music and that the management of the company would be performing at a high level, but all other things being equal, the incentive program had a huge impact on our client's business.

Oh! And by the way, when they returned from the trip, the client bought the back cover of the industry magazine to thank Ethan and his team! (Yes, the second major, publicized "thank you" from the client!)

Those were intangible impacts, but there were also tangible *measurements* of the impact of this incentive trip that I will now share to conclude this chapter.

Measurement of the Tangible

I already described the context of the music industry in the late nineties and at the beginning of this century. In addition to the dropping market shares, you found fierce competition and a total change in the business model with artists starting to focus more on live performances before anything else. In that context, Ethan and I wanted to *measure* the impact of the company's incentive campaign. We had the intangible, but we needed to add the tangible.

Over the course of two years, between 1998 and 2000, we compiled three types of data provided by Ethan and put them on three curves: (1) the market, (2) revenue from clients not participating in the incentive program, and (3) revenue from the clients participating in the incentive program. The results were undisputable:

- Ethan's company outperformed the market, which is a testimonial to the quality of the artists they represented and the albums they produced but also indicates the high quality of the company's management.

- Even more interesting, the revenue from clients participating in the incentive program constantly outperformed the revenue from those not participating in the incentive program.

Those statistics confirmed the figures mentioned in previous chapters about the impact of incentive business. Even still, I want to illustrate the ease and value of *measuring* the impact of a world-class face-to-face.

BIG Chapter Takeaways

Once again, there is so much that could be written on the *measurement* part. What we have to remember is:

- One, to *identify* exactly the objective of the meeting.

- Two, to *identify* what we're going to *measure*.

- Three, to *identify* how we're going to *measure* that, and obviously ...

- Four, to prepare the reporting back to the different stakeholders involved in the decision-making process and by doing so, to be able to link the specific event to the company's strategy and its *execution*.

Next Up

Now that your face-to-face meeting is over and you have *measured* its impact, you need to think about the *follow-up*.

Obvious? Perhaps, but think twice—how many times have you purposely and consciously planned a strategic *follow-up* to a face-to-face meeting? That's what we are going to discuss in the next chapter.

Chapter 6: Follow Up

Not following up with your prospects is the same as filling up your bathtub without first putting the stopper in the drain.

—from *Selling Simplified* by Michelle Moore

I could have named this chapter "Extend the Benefits of Your Meeting," but "Follow Up" is even better in that it encompasses all the various touchpoints with your stakeholders that happen after the meeting.

You have mobilized a lot of resources to organize your face-to-face meeting. You have carefully planned the communication before the meeting and have managed to go beyond your attendees' expectations. Then ... everybody goes home, and the next day at the office, it is business as usual, almost as if nothing had really happened. What a waste of money and missed opportunity!

As I have said before, to solve any major corporate challenge, you will always find a face-to-face meeting down the road. Will it be enough? No! Will you be able to solve your challenge without it? No! So why would you stop at the end of the meeting? Unfortunately, that happens more than it should because from the beginning of the planning process, you haven't thought about the "after the meeting" part. Here are five examples to illustrate my point.

Example 1—Back to Luc and His Kick-off Meeting

In chapter 2, I shared the example of the kick-off meeting during which Luc helped his colleagues visualize their daily work when the new strategy—including the Internet—would be in place by dramatizing it, instead of "just explaining the strategy" in a speech or PowerPoint presentation. This kick-off meeting also reassured everyone that despite the introduction of the Internet in all the processes, everybody was going to keep their jobs.

A very important element that made the whole meeting so successful was the *follow-up*. From the beginning, we had planned the "next week after the meeting" process for the client, and this is what happened.

Each department head had already planned her or his team meeting following the kick-off and started the meeting by explaining, "First of all, you have seen that we are all keeping our jobs. Second of all, you have seen where we are going and what our daily jobs will look like in two years when the entire strategy will have been implemented. Now, let's work backwards.

Let's see what it means for our department, what the milestones are, and who is going to do what."

This is an example of effective *follow-up*, of leveraging the power of the meeting and extending its benefits beyond the meeting. This would have never been possible without our having *designed* both the face-to-face AND the *follow-up* beforehand.

Example 2—Follow-up in regard to Advisory Boards

Another concrete example of the importance of the *follow-up* relates to advisory boards. Whether it's a strategic advisory board or a customer advisory board, you're basically gathering people who are giving you their time. Sometimes they will be compensated or paid, but what they do in most cases is give you their time to reflect on your challenges, to reflect on your strategy, and to share with you ideas.

Accordingly, the least you should do is really update them on the important findings from the meeting and what you are planning to do or not to do. It has to be made very clear from the beginning that regardless of what they're going to recommend, the ultimate decision about implementing their recommendations will be in your hands. Even still it's also good for them to know what you took out of the meeting, what your main learning was, and what you are planning to do about the issue at hand.

In the weeks *following* the advisory board, you should send them an executive summary of the outcomes of the meeting. Then at the next meeting, you should update them on the results, what has been implemented, what worked, what didn't, etc. It is the best way to keep them engaged and committed to you and to your organization.

Example 3—Following Up in the Favela

In this example, I'm sharing an amazing experience, which took place in Rio de Janeiro. We all know that Rio is beautiful. It's a city that has amazing opportunities to create unique experiences, but one of the highlights of the program actually happened in a favela, which can be understood as "a slum in Brazil, within urban areas"![17]

Tom was an amazing general manager, with a clear vision for his business, and a deep sense of corporate responsibility. In order to contribute to a charity, "just writing a check" wasn't an option for Tom! Tom's financial donation had to serve a purpose, to bring more value than just a one-time donation.

We had planned from the beginning that we were going to spend half a day and lunch in a favela. You have to know that this favela is actually supported by the city of Rio, which built a lift that goes from the city up to the favela so that people can come and go easily, not needing hours to move from the city to the favela and vice versa. Obviously with the lift in place, it creates opportunities for residents of the favela to be able to work in the city and visit the city for activities. With the lift, favela residents are not so isolated.

In this favela, people have also been investing in education and have created a school where kids can learn to dance, play music, and later on, continue their learning to find a job in their field.

Because Tom was looking for a meaningful area for his company to donate money, we discussed with our local partner the school's needs. Something the school needed was an Internet connection so that students could take advantage of online courses as well as remotely study languages with teachers abroad.

Tom ended up organizing a fundraiser with the incentive winners, and the company matched the amount the fundraiser was able to collect!

The next day, attendees presented a big check to the school to pay for Internet and online language courses. It was during this school visit that the attendees had the most memorable experience. We were warmly welcomed by the students and teachers, and we enjoyed an outstanding show put on by the students with dance and music. Their enthusiasm was absolutely amazing, and we ended up in a mini-carnival where the band, the favela residents, and the attendees were all dancing in the streets as they walked us to the big lift.

It was a unique moment, a unique experience that the attendees still remember to this day.

The company used this special experience at the school in their *follow-up* communications with the attendees. After the participants returned to work, the company reminded them that thanks to their fundraising and donation to the school, they were able to impact durably and significantly the lives of those young people, all the while enjoying a superb destination.

The two final examples I want to share involve meetings that took place in Africa, more specifically in Tanzania and Zimbabwe.

Example 4—The Maasaï Perspective

I was with a client on an incentive trip that we'd organized in Olduvaï, Tanzania, spending two days with the Maasaï while enjoying a camp of luxury en-suite tents. You could look 360 degrees around and not see one building, not even one telephone line. The nature was splendid, and we found ourselves on a little mound overlooking the Serengeti. Naserian, one of the Maasaï warriors who was escorting us in case we encountered lions, looked at me and started the conversation:

Naserian: Eric, do you know the difference between the Swiss and us?

Eric: Not really ... What is it?

Naserian: The Swiss have watches ... We, the Maasaï, have time!

I think the Serengeti still resonates from my laugh! It was an amazing exchange that I never miss quoting and one which I actually have used many times in my cross-cultural training sessions.

It is also the type of quote or example that produces a lasting memory—one that is easy to share and repeat in *follow-up*. For that reason, we always try to incorporate it in any program so that you, the senior executive, can make reference to it in your subsequent meetings as a way to extend the benefits of your incentive trip.

To finish this chapter with a last example about the importance of *follow-up*, let's leave Tanzania, fly south over Mozambique, and land in Zimbabwe.

Example 5—Thirteen, Our Lucky Number!

You might remember Ethan and his major company in the music industry that I wrote about in the previous chapter. The first incentive program we organized for his company's clients took place in Zimbabwe in 1998. The summer before, as we were preparing all the details, I realized that we were going to be there on Friday the 13th of February, 1998 and that we'd scheduled rafting to happen on Saturday February 14. I also realized that the following March the 13th ... was also a Friday! So, I suggested that we move the rafting activity to Friday the 13th of February. Bear with me until the end!

If you have the great opportunity to go on a rafting journey in Victoria Falls, you will enjoy the Zambezi River, you will enjoy a magnificent BBQ by the river for lunch, and you will play volleyball on real sand before re-boarding your raft and finishing the course. The whole experience is stimulating, but the most challenging moment is when you have to walk up the gorges of the Zambezi River. It is steep and takes about thirty minutes, so when you arrive at the top— you are totally cooked!

So, on Friday the 13th of February, 1998, we did exactly that, and when everyone had arrived at the top of the gorges, we took a group picture.

A month later, on Friday the 13th of March, 1998, each client received the group picture with a note from Ethan: "Don't worry, every Friday the 13th, you won't have to climb out of the gorges of the Zambezi River!"

To this day, every time there is a Friday the 13th, the attendees all remember their experience on the Zambezi! That is extending the benefits of the meeting in the future! Talk about a powerful *follow-up*!

BIG Chapter Takeaways

Whatever the type of meeting you are implementing, the investment you are making in it deserves to be extended as much as possible into the future. It's easy if you plan it out from the beginning. Unfortunately, these beneficial *follow-ups* tend to be overlooked by those in the C-suite!

However, now that I've shared with you the benefits of *following up* and given you several examples of high impact *follow-ups*, as well as their benefits, you are well prepared to incorporate *following up* into your face-to-face methodology.

Next Up

A common mistake is to try to always do something "more expensive," something "better, just to top the previous year." That path leads to a dead end! Rather than aiming to spend a lot of money or outdo the previous year's meeting, look at doing something "different"—that's the key to success and to a sustainable approach to face-to-face. Looking to do it *uniquely different* is the key to *executing* a meeting with the greatest impact. This is what the last part is all about—doing it again, *uniquely different*.

Chapter 7: Uniquely Different

And now here is my secret, a very simple secret: It is only with the heart that one can see rightly; what is essential is invisible to the eye.

—from *The Little Prince* by Antoine de Saint-Exupéry

I remember once hearing somebody remark, "Yeah, I brought my team together. I did an incentive trip. It really didn't work."

When I asked what they'd done on the trip, it was basically bringing people to a nice hotel, having a welcome cocktail, followed by dinner. In between, there were boring sessions or ... nothing except people hanging out on the beach.

Quite frankly, a trip like that is a waste of money. It is a waste of time. It is a waste of energy. Most importantly, it is not leveraging the power of a meeting.

All successful companies that really leverage the power of their meetings, and do so successfully, always look to having *uniquely different* content, at a *uniquely different* location, with *uniquely different* programs and *uniquely different* speakers because at the end of the day, the opportunities to do something *uniquely different* are limitless.

The problem is that people are not thinking about the complete process that I've presented in the previous chapters. They don't look at the company's strategy. They don't look at *understanding* the different stakeholders and *identifying* them. They don't *identify* the single, pressing objective of the meeting. They don't think about the complete picture of the meeting and instead are concerned only with whether to stay internal or hire external people to put the logistics together. That's where their thinking and planning starts and ends. There's little to no consideration of the event's content, its why, and the expected outcomes.

It comes as no surprise then that afterwards they think that the event didn't really work, and they're not happy with it.

If you were my boss and you promised me, "Eric, if you work hard, then you're going to attend the most incredible sales meeting or you're going to participate in an amazing program or you're going to live out a unique experience." And then at the end, after having worked so hard, I only experienced a basic event that I could duplicate with my family or friends—where is the leverage? Where is the excitement? Where is the learning? Where is the incentive?

Quite frankly, where is the opportunity for me to speak about it to those around me who ask, "How was it?"? My response would be, "Yeah, well, it was okay."

Then the next time you, as my boss, come to me and promise, "This year, if you work hard, we're going to do something unique," then I'm going to look at you and reply, "You know what—I heard that last year ... whatever." I'm not going to be committed. I'm not going to be inspired. And probably, no one else will be either.

As a corporate executive, you should really be thinking through the whole process and creating *uniquely different* experiences. Then you can be sure that the people participating will be making every effort to return the following year. They will want to be part of the program. They will be talking about it to those around them. Their colleagues will also want to participate. The event will build drive and momentum among attendees, and the revenue of your company will likely reap the benefits from that enthusiasm and dedication.

Do What the Successful Companies Do

You should already know that there are very successful companies that think strategically about their events.

One client company that organizes a bi-annual retreat has never been twice to the same location in ten years.

They have never done twice the same type of activities, and they have never set up the same type of agenda or the same format for their working sessions. Every year, the participants' feedback is: "This was amazing, you won't be able to top that!" And they don't look to top it—they look to do something *uniquely different* each time.

Another example that comes to mind is the many customer events that we've put together for a coffee distribution company. For years, we would take care of the customer events. Most of the time, it would host the same 60 to 80 percent of the attendees from previous years, so it was crucial not to do the same thing. This was possible. Not only was it possible, but the world offers so many opportunities that it's not that difficult.

The world is vast, the opportunities are endless, new venues are being built or renovated, and there is always something new happening. In other words, besides your content, the location, the venue, or its history always present opportunities to build an unforgettable and *uniquely different* program.

Take, for instance, the Park Hyatt Paris-Vendôme. Besides the impeccable service, the façade of the hotel has a totally amazing history. It is made of two different façades, one of which has been elevated (yes, you read correctly—elevated) so as to appear as one uniform façade. You should see the pictures of how it was built. When we explained it to the clients, they couldn't believe it. We even arranged for them to tour the neighborhood around the hotel, and they ended up in Coco Chanel's apartment with a look-a-like welcoming everyone and talking about her life—another unforgettable moment punctuating a full day of working sessions.

What you need before anything else is the mindset, the willingness to follow the process and to create experiences that people cannot duplicate—experiences that are *uniquely different*.

Big Chapter Takeaways

At the end of the day, you want something *uniquely different*, not "something more" or "bigger." You want to offer a *uniquely different* experience that meets the objectives of the meeting, which speaks to the hearts and minds of the participants, and which most importantly, helps the organization to *execute* meetings that increase business performance.

Next Up

We have now come full circle with the 7-part methodology and, before you close this book, I have one wish for you.

My Parting Wish for You

Face-to-face meetings are critical to any organization's success. From advisory boards to sales meetings, from trade shows to incentive travel, each serves a purpose and plays a specific role in the *execution* of your company's strategy.

Logistics are very important but need to serve a higher purpose. There is a logical process to follow: Understand – Identify – Design – Execute – Measure – Follow Up – and Uniquely Different. These seven steps allow those following them to enjoy amazing results.

To reach that level though, we need a new type of leader. We need individuals who will focus first on the success of their organization and who will think beyond what I call "the compliance syndrome": too many people are more concerned about being compliant than about taking risks. They prefer to do "business as usual" rather than offer innovative solutions. They tend to ask themselves questions, such as "If I do this or say that, will I risk getting fired?" instead of asking, "Is this good for my company and will it differentiate us from the competition?"

We need C-level executives who truly believe that people are the greatest assets of their organization and who understand how to touch people's hearts and minds.

We need C-level executives who leverage the power of face-to-face meetings to address their business challenges: alignment, engagement, motivation, networking, education, and customer relationships.

We need C-level executives who will think first about the objectives and the content, and then about the logistics.

We need C-level executives who understand that face-to-face meetings are the greatest management tool they could and should use.

We need C-level executives who know when to get involved and when to delegate.

We need C-level executives who understand the power of meetings and who realize that meetings mean business.

We need clever C-level executives who are willing to do something other than the same old stuff—and instead, seek to do something *uniquely different*!

As I'm airborne somewhere between Los Angeles and Miami, finishing the last lines of this book, I'm grateful to be working in the meetings and events industry. I know how greatly we support organizations, and I'm proud of how much we bring to our country in terms of job opportunities and federal, state, and local taxes.[18]

In this book, through one example after another, I have explained why and how to *execute* a remarkable event.

Now it is up to you to implement it.

I wish you good luck and leave you with the wise words of Master Yoda: "Do or do not, there is no try!"

BONUS: EXPERT ARTICLE

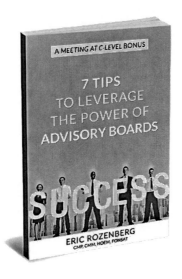

https://swantegy.leadpages.co/7-tips/

Make your Advisory Board more effective!

Download the "7 Tips to Leverage the Power of Advisory Boards" and start getting next-level feedback from your advisors.

Acknowledgments

To Vimari Roman in Miami, Florida—this book exists because of you and your persistence in asking me to write it! Thank you for your friendship and partnership. The future looks good!

To Georges Yana in Brussels, Belgium—your wisdom, intelligence, integrity, and experience were instrumental in developing the methodology explained in this book, which we have been using for years. Thank you for everything.

To Kevin Olsen in Chicago, Illinois—thank you for your friendship, your partnership, and your vision. You are a great family man and entrepreneur.

To all the clients and local partners around the world who trust me and with whom I enjoy doing business— I hope I will never have to start working!

To all my meetings and events industry friends and colleagues—I continue to learn from you every day. Thank you for making ours the greatest industry to work in.

To Ramy Vance—for amazing coaching during the writing process and launch.

To Nancy Pile—for transforming my "foreign English" into "native English." Thank you for all your editing work.

References

1. "Business Leaders Survey Key Findings," Meetings Mean Business, accessed April 15, 2016, http://www.meetingsmeanbusiness.com/sites/defaul t/files/MMB%20Business%20Leaders%20Survey%20 Key%20Findings.pdf.

2. Ibid.

3. Bill McDermott, *Winners Dream: A Journey from Corner Store to Corner Office* (New York, NY: Simon and Schuster, 2014).

4. "Bill McDermott Winners Dream Press Conference at IMEX America 2014 – (5 minute extract)," YouTube, October 24, 2014, accessed April 15, 2016, https://www.youtube.com/watch?v=QZnso8lJBuQ&f eature=youtu.be.

5. Lewis Carroll, *Alice in Wonderland* (London: Macmillan, 1865).

6. William A. Schiemann, "Aligning Performance Management with Organizational Strategy, Values, and Goals," in *Performance Management: Putting*

Research into Action, ed. James W. Smither and Manuel London (San Francisco, CA: John Wiley and Sons, Inc., 2009), 45–88.

7. "Non-Cash Incentives: Best Practices to Optimize Sales Effectiveness," Incentive Research Foundation, February 26, 2013, accessed April 15, 2016, http://theirf.org/research/non-cash-incentives-best-practices-to-optimize-sales-effectiveness/183/.

8. "Rewards and Recognition as a Vital Compensation Component," Incentive Research Foundation, February 21, 2012, accessed April 15, 2016, http://theirf.org/research/rewards-and-recognition-as-a-vital-compensation-component/193/.

9. "US Business Use of Incentive Travel Awards," Incentive Research Foundation, September 10, 2014, accessed April 15, 2016, http://theirf.org/research/us-business-use-of-incentive-travel-awards/1289.

10. Ibid.

11. Ibid.

12. "The Most Stressful Jobs of 2016," CareerCast, accessed April 17, 2016, http://www.careercast.com/jobs-rated/most-stressful-jobs-2016.

13. "Hurricane Jeanne," Wikipedia, the Free Encyclopedia, last modified March 9, 2016, accessed April 17, 2016, https://en.wikipedia.org/wiki/Hurricane_Jeanne.

14. "Jack Phillips," ROI Institute, accessed April 17, 2016, http://www.roiinstitute.net/jack-phillips/.

15. "DreamForce," Salesforce.com, accessed April 17, 2016, http://www.salesforce.com/dreamforce/DF15/.

16. "Sapphire Now + ASUG Annual Conference," SAP, accessed April 17, 2016, http://events.sap.com/sapandasug/en/home.html?bc=1.

17. "Favela," Wikipedia, the Free Encyclopedia, last modified April 6, 2016, accessed April 17, 2016, https://en.wikipedia.org/wiki/Favela.

18. According to a recent study by PricewaterhouseCoopers ("Economic Significance Study," Convention Industry Council, accessed April 17, 2016, http://www.conventionindustry.org/ResearchInfo/EconomicSignificanceStudy.aspx.), the meetings industry contributed more than $280 billion to the national economy and put another $88 billion back into the economy through federal, state, and local taxes in 2012.

About the Author

Eric Rozenberg, CMP, CMM, HOEM, FONSAT, is an entrepreneur, speaker, and author who helps organizations in the execution of their strategies. He is president of Swantegy (www.swantegy.com) and a founding partner of Keyway (www.thekeyway.com).

He started to travel the world and interact with other cultures while studying business, thanks to AIESEC (the largest student association in the world). He has worked in over fifty countries and speaks several languages. He was the first European to become chairman of the international board of Meetings Professional International (MPI) and is a current member of Entrepreneurs' Organization (EO).

When not sleeping in a plane or a hotel, he enjoys his family and the paradise of South Florida.

You can reach him via LinkedIn (www.linkedin.com /in/eric-rozenberg-652199).

CPSIA information can be obtained
at www.ICGtesting.com
Printed in the USA
LVOW10s0521191017
552970LV00004B/403/P